Reading First

Eight practice tests for the **Cambridge B2 First**, Paper 1

Monica Ruda-Peachey

PROSPERITY EDUCATION

PROSPERITY EDUCATION
www.prosperityeducation.net

Registered offices: Sherlock Close, Cambridge
CB3 0HP, United Kingdom

© Prosperity Education Ltd. 2020

First published 2020

ISBN: 978-1-91-612974-0

Manufactured on demand by KDP.

For further information and resources, visit:
www.prosperityeducation.net

To infinity and beyond.

Contents

Bonus content from *Use of English: ten practice tests for the Cambridge B2 First*

Introduction

Welcome to this edition of sample tests for the Cambridge B2 First, Reading (Parts 5–7).

This resource comprises eight whole Reading tests, answer keys, write-in answer sheets and a marking scheme, allowing you to score each test out of 23 marks.

Author Monica Ruda-Peachey is a DELTA-qualified ELT writer, teacher and Trinity TESOL teacher-trainer. She has designed and delivered training sessions for in-house and external teacher-training workshops and courses, and her articles have been published in print and online by major ELT journals (*English Teaching Professional* and *IATEFL Voices*).

The content has been written to closely replicate the Cambridge exam experience, and has undergone comprehensive review. You or your students, if you are a teacher, will hopefully enjoy the wide range of essay topics and benefit from the repetitive practice, something that is key to preparing for this part of the B2 First (FCE) examination.

For me, having prepared many students for this and other Cambridge exams, pre- and post-2015, when the specification changed, it is Paper 1 that poses the biggest challenge. Without there being much support available by way of quality practice material, students struggle to gain the necessary levels of confidence in the Use of English and Reading section prior to sitting the exam. Therefore, in my classes, after studying and working through the core knowledge required, we drill, drill and drill exercises in preparation for the exams.

I hope that you will find this resource a useful study aid, and I wish you all the best in preparing for the exam.

Michael Macdonald
Madrid, 2020

Visit www.prosperityeducation.net to view our wide range of Cambridge resources.

Cambridge B2 First Reading: Parts 5–7

Test 1

You are going to read an extract from a novel in which a woman called Jade talks about a wedding. For questions 31–36, read the text and decide which answer fits best according to the text. In the separate answer sheet, mark the appropriate answer (A, B, C or D).

All the guests were going to be there soon, but Jade hadn't finished yet. She had been preparing this wedding for a while and wanted everything to be perfect. Although it wasn't her wedding, she felt just as nervous as a bride – it was her first project as a wedding planner. She could hardly contain her excitement in spite of everyone's doubt. Her family members had never believed that she would actually leave her stable 9–5 job to pursue such a financially unpredictable career until she announced it.

It was a sunny Sunday afternoon at her parents' house. Jade knew they would have all been there at that time. She and her brothers were chatting while watching TV; their mum and dad were playing cards, enjoying each other's company. Suddenly, Jade stood up and shyly but proudly shared her news: she had resigned from her well-paid job as a personal assistant to dedicate herself to becoming a wedding planner.

The whole family stood still. They all just sat there, staring at her and shaking their heads in disapproval. Her mother had a worried look in her eyes, while her father was clearly disappointed. Jade's brothers broke the silence by asking questions: *Do you know what you are doing? How are you going to find clients? Why do you think this is a good idea?* Their reaction didn't come as a surprise to Jade. Her family had never been supportive of her dreams and ambitions. They thought that work was all she cared about, but they wished she had a conventional lifestyle. She was 37 years old and not only did she have no intention of getting married, but she also had no wish to become a mother. Jade had rejected all the goals that her parents had set for her.

But at that point, their opinion didn't matter. After all, they had never pushed themselves out of their comfort zones. None of them had ever tried anything new in their life because they had
Line 23 always played it safe. Her parents' disappointment, her brother's disbelief, her ex-employer's doubts were a distant memory. She knew what she wanted and she was going to achieve it. It wasn't going to be easy, and there were going to be ups and downs, but she was confident that her business would be a success. In that moment, all that mattered was the outcome of that wedding that Jade had been planning – together with the bride and the groom – for months. The flowers had already been arranged on the tables and all around the room by the florist, the delicious food was ready to be served by waiters wearing impeccable uniforms, and musicians, who were tuning their instruments, were ready to entertain the guests.

Only the cake was missing… The wedding cake hadn't been delivered yet! Jade immediately called the bakery to find out what had happened. There had been an accident on the road that slowed down the traffic – the cake was on its way. While she was on the phone, the delivery van arrived at the venue. There it was! The cake had finally arrived and Jade heaved a sigh of relief. She couldn't even begin to imagine what would have happened if the cake hadn't turned up. Without a doubt, the bride would have been in tears, the groom would have been extremely angry and Jade's career would have ended in a flash.

Everything was finally ready. As the musicians started to play their cheerful music, the guests began to arrive. Everyone was talking, but the atmosphere was tense. Some seemed shocked, some seemed upset, in contrast with the music. Something must have happened at the ceremony and she hadn't been informed. Jade had desperately tried to find the bride and groom, but there was no sign of either of them. There was the mother of the bride, crying on her husband's shoulder. There was the father of the groom shouting at his one and only son. Something must have gone terribly wrong. Selfishly, Jade thought about the effect that might have had on her business. Would they have recommended her services to other clients? Luckily, they had already settled the payment, so she didn't need to worry about the money.

31   In the first paragraph, why is Jade nervous?

   A   Because she is the bride at this wedding.

   B   Because she has left her job.

   C   Because she is starting her own business.

   D   Because her family doesn't support her financially.

32   In paragraph 2, Jade makes her announcement on a Sunday afternoon because:

   A   her family members hardly ever see each other.

   B   her family members are all together.

   C   her brothers are in a good mood.

   D   her mum and dad aren't busy.

33   In the third paragraph, Jade's family doesn't support her dreams because they:

   A   want Jade to have a traditional lifestyle.

   B   want Jade to spend more time with them.

   C   think Jade works too much.

   D   believe Jade is too ambitious.

34   In line 23, 'played it safe' means:

   A   they prefer playing cards instead of going to work.

   B   they want to live in a comfortable area.

   C   they are always careful, avoiding risks.

   D   they don't want to leave a safe environment.

35   In the fifth paragraph, why does Jade call the bakery?

   A   To defend her reputation.

   B   To reassure the bride and the groom.

   C   To find out who was involved in the accident.

   D   To assess the location of the cake.

36   In paragraph 6, as they arrive, the guests look:

   A   as cheerful as the music.

   B   tired from the long ceremony.

   C   ready to eat the delicious food.

   D   unhappy and confused.

You are going to read a newspaper article in which the writer talks about the lives of hermits. Six sentences have been removed. For questions 37–42, read the text and choose from options A–G the sentence that fits each gap. There is one extra sentence that you do not need to use.

Who Needs Modern Society?

A quick look into the lives of those choosing to avoid human connection

In this day and age, it is not uncommon for people to feel overwhelmed by their everyday life. **37** On the other hand, there is a small number of people, called hermits, who decide to abandon modern society completely, separating themselves from the rest of the world. However, when we think of a hermit, we often envisage a wise old man living in a cave, but that is hardly ever the case. The truth is that no two hermits are alike.

There are various reasons why some individuals choose this unconventional lifestyle. Often, technology, stress and work overload can be factors that contribute to becoming a recluse. **38** Another difference can be noticed regarding their background, which is not necessarily a religious one. Modern hermits come from all walks of life. Just like any of us, most of them had a conventional lifestyle – some used to be teachers, social workers, business people.

The main aspect that differentiates one hermit from another is the level of isolation they choose to embrace. While some of these individuals live in complete isolation, others meet family and friends occasionally to maintain some sort of human connection. Some hermits keep up to date with the world around them by surfing the internet and making contact with others by communicating on social platforms.

Regardless of the type and level of isolation, basic human needs have to be met to ensure survival. **39** Some of those who reject every aspect of modern society often choose to build their own house, usually a basic shelter made of wood far from urban areas. Others live in caravans or in small rustic cottages. When it comes to feeding themselves, most hermits grow their own vegetables and keep chickens for eggs, while some forage berries and mushrooms that grow in the wild.

Although they lead a very simple life, being a hermit can be financially challenging. **40** Modern hermits are very resourceful in finding creative ways to pay for their household expenses. Some choose to work from home, providing proof-reading and editorial services, engaging in craft work or web design. The internet offers plenty of work opportunities that don't require leaving the house. Another way to self-support a reclusive lifestyle is by taking on casual or part-time employment away from home that occupies only a small proportion of their time. **41** In fact, it is quite common to take advantage of savings or state pensions to finance a reclusive lifestyle.

Avoiding face-to-face human connection for long periods of time might seem challenging to us, but it brings some advantages. **42** In addition, it provides opportunities for physical and mental relaxation, away from people's negativity.

All in all, becoming a recluse is a choice that requires hard work and dedication. While spending some time alone going on a spiritual or relaxing retreat might be appealing for many, long periods of isolation are often difficult to endure for most of us.

A   Many modern hermits use funds and assets acquired before entering a life of solitude for the purpose of supporting it.

B   However, religious, spiritual and moral beliefs are frequently the cause of this unusual choice.

C   Solitude plays a key role in the life of a hermit, who might feel lonely sometimes.

D   Hermits have to work hard to get what we often take for granted, such as a roof over our heads and food on our tables.

E   First of all, it is believed that being alone increases creativity and sharpens the ability to focus.

F   To escape this fast-paced living, most of us can have a relaxing break in the countryside, go on holiday, or take up a hobby to reduce our stress levels.

G   The biggest obstacle to an isolated life is figuring out how to sustain it.

You are going to read four people's accounts of recent restaurant experiences. For questions 43–52, read the text below and, in the separate answer sheet, choose the correct paragraph (A–D).

The 'pleasure' of eating out
Dining out should be an enjoyable experience, not a stressful one!

A As soon as we walked through the doors of this newly decorated restaurant, I knew I had picked the wrong place for a romantic evening with my girlfriend. Both floors of the restaurant were incredibly busy, as there were several birthday parties going on. The noise levels were so high that we could hardly hear each other speak. Extra tables were added to make room for more customers and I had to move my chair every time a waiter needed to reach another table! A busy restaurant is usually a sign of good food. Unfortunately, this wasn't the case. Our meal wasn't bad, but it definitely wasn't memorable either. The food was very basic and the portions were quite small. We also waited 20 minutes for our bill, but I finally had a nice surprise – it was very cheap, and that's why this restaurant is so popular.

B Don't be fooled by its elegant furniture and glamorous design – service in this restaurant is a true disappointment. It was a special event for me and my family, so I wanted everything to be perfect. I had already paid a deposit to ensure our evening would run smoothly. Having booked our table weeks in advance, I was confident that it would be ready on our arrival. Instead, we had to wait almost an hour to be seated. The waitress brought us our drinks, but at that point we were really hungry and we quickly placed our food order. We were looking forward to our dinner, which was very good, but again, we had to wait about 45 minutes to be served. I won't be eating there again, even though the food is nice.

C My best friend knows about my passion for exotic food and took me for a meal at this glorious restaurant. Its neon green and yellow sign above the door wasn't exactly appealing, giving it a cheap and cheerful kind of look, but I didn't let it stop me and I went in. Well, I'm so glad I did! The atmosphere was friendly and relaxed. The waiting staff wore their traditional oriental costumes, instead of boring uniforms. Our waiter took the time to introduce himself and tell us about the history of the restaurant. He had to translate the menu for us, as it was written in a language we couldn't read. You couldn't fault the service, nor the quality of the food. Although some western options were available, I wanted to try their most traditional cuisine. Each dish was beautifully presented and cooked to the highest standards. This was a fantastic all-round dining experience that I won't forget!

D It was my mum's 60th birthday and there were 25 people at our table. The service was good and the food was lovely. We were all having a great time! I was going to settle the bill at the end of our meal. To make the payment more manageable, I had already paid a large deposit to the manager when I booked our table. As planned, when we were ready to leave, I wanted to pay. Checking the bill, I noticed that it was much more expensive than expected. I explained about the deposit we had already paid, but the staff knew nothing about it. I asked to speak to the manager, but I was told he had resigned and had left just that week. It became clear to me that the manager had run away with my deposit money. The assistant manager, however, was very sympathetic towards my situation. We didn't have to pay for the missing sum in the end.

Which paragraph mentions a restaurant that:

is not suitable for a quiet and private dinner?	43
gives a negative first impression from the outside?	44
wasn't prepared for the customers?	45
had a very slow service?	46
was uncomfortable and overcrowded?	47
was let down by a former member of staff?	48
made a positive, long-lasting impression on the writer?	49
served Asian food?	50
showed understanding towards a customer's issue?	51
served average food?	52

Answer sheet: Cambridge B2 First Reading

Test No. [   ]

Mark out of 23 [   ]

Name _____   Date _____

Part 5   *6 marks*

Mark the appropriate answer (A, B, C or D).

| 0 | A | B | **C** | D | |

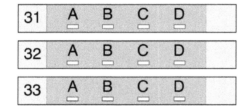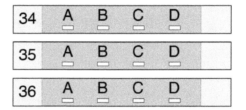

31	A	B	C	D			34	A	B	C	D	
32	A	B	C	D			35	A	B	C	D	
33	A	B	C	D			36	A	B	C	D	

Part 6   *7 marks*

Add the appropriate answer (A–G).

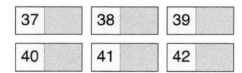

| 37 | | 38 | | 39 | |
| 40 | | 41 | | 42 | |

Part 7   *10 marks*

Add the appropriate answer (A, B, C or D).

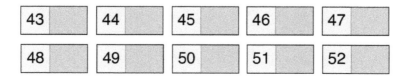

| 43 | | 44 | | 45 | | 46 | | 47 | |
| 48 | | 49 | | 50 | | 51 | | 52 | |

Cambridge B2 First Reading: Parts 5–7

Test 2

You are going to read an extract from a novel in which a woman called Esther talks about working at a summer camp. For questions 31–36, read the text and decide which answer fits best according to the text. In the separate answer sheet, mark the appropriate answer (A, B, C or D).

My first time working at a summer camp was ten years ago, when I had just turned 18. At that time, I didn't find the idea of spending my summer days looking after noisy kids very appealing. I wasn't a sociable teenager and I had only two friends. They were amazing, but they were the complete opposite of me. Both of them were social butterflies! They enjoyed playing beach volleyball and meeting new people. They also loved parties! My friends were always invited to the best parties in town because they were so popular, unlike me, but I didn't mind that. I was happy to spend time alone in my room listening to music or watching videos online.

Unfortunately, my parents didn't like the idea of me being on my own so often. So, that year, on my last day of school before the summer holidays, they gave me two options – both equally scary for me: I could either spend my school break going out with my friends every day or I could spend it working. Even just the thought of going out and meeting people for weeks on end was too much for me. Finding a job and making some money, instead of spending it, sounded like a much better alternative.

Luckily, my parents were really pleased with my choice and admired my sense of responsibility. They were extremely supportive, but their enthusiasm for my summer job soon turned into obsession. Every morning, they would check online for local job vacancies and would email companies and businesses asking for vacant positions. They even wrote my CV! I applied for many jobs, but I received hardly any replies. My young age and lack of work experience apparently weren't what employers were looking for. One morning, however, I woke up to a very friendly email from the director of a summer camp offering me a place as a camp entertainer. There were promises of new friendships, fun-filled days and endless learning opportunities while looking after young children.

I didn't know whether to laugh or cry. I didn't actually think that anyone would offer me a job, especially one involving looking after kids! Working with children requires so much patience and energy... and it's such a huge responsibility! What if something happens to them? What a frightening thought! On the other hand, I was excited to do something new. New things are always scary, of course, but I was now ready for a summer of adventures. I felt I finally had a purpose in life, and doing something meaningful had to be better than wasting my days on the beach like my friends do every year.

As soon as I got to the camp, I was introduced to ten other entertainers. I hadn't thought about working with other staff members when I accepted the job. Did I really think it was going to be just the children and me? I thought that, having left my friends behind, I had escaped social situations, but now I would have to chat with complete strangers! Making conversation always made me nervous, especially with people I didn't know, so I came up with a plan. I decided to keep away from everybody as much as possible, and to dedicate all my time to the children – that's what I was there for, after all!

Obviously, my plan didn't work. By the end of my second day at the camp I had already met all the other entertainers and found myself talking with some of them at every break. The camp director wasn't lying when he promised fun, friendship and learning opportunities. I soon felt I had become a part of a team and that this camp experience had a lot to offer. During my eight weeks at the camp, no two days were the same. I was involved in the organisation of games and activities for the children, while making sure they were always safe, and I learnt to be responsible for others and to help those who need me. The most important lesson I learnt, however, is that sharing life experiences with good friends is a lot
Line 46 more enjoyable than going through them on your own.

31   In the first paragraph, what is Esther's main point?

   A   She would like to be as popular as her friends.

   B   She does not like spending time with her friends.

   C   She expresses her desire to find a summer job.

   D   She gives a description of her personality.

32   In the second paragraph, Esther chooses to:

   A   enjoy her summer with her friends.

   B   earn some money finding a summer job.

   C   spend her money with her friends.

   D   spend her summer break on her own.

33   In paragraph 3, why is it difficult for Esther to get a job?

   A   Because mature employees with experience are preferred.

   B   Because she doesn't check her emails.

   C   Because her parents wrote her CV.

   D   Because employers aren't offering any jobs at the moment.

34   In the fourth paragraph, how does Esther feel about the job offer?

   A   She is terrified of working with children.

   B   She is excited about spending her summer away from her friends.

   C   She has mixed feelings about it.

   D   She thinks it would be better to be at the beach with her friends.

35   In paragraph 5, when she arrives at the camp, Esther realises that:

   A   she is going to be alone with the children for a long period of time.

   B   she is going to work as a part of a team.

   C   the staff members are trying to make her feel nervous.

   D   she needs a plan to work at the camp.

36   In the last paragraph, what does 'them' refers to in line 46?

   A   Good friends

   B   Life experiences

   C   Learning opportunities

   D   Games and activities for children

You are going to read a newspaper article in which the writer talks about the relationship between dogs and people. Six sentences have been removed. For questions 37–42, read the text and choose from options A–G the sentence that fits each gap. There is one extra sentence that you do not need to use.

A Man's Best Friend

Learn more about your pet dog for a happy friendship

What a warm feeling it is to be greeted by a wagging tail after a hard day's work! Dogs are loyal creatures that give unconditional love and can provide companionship to their human friends. They don't care about physical appearance and don't think about the past or worry about the future. **37** For this reason, looking after a dog can help people develop a sense of responsibility and improve their appreciation for life. Perhaps that's why dogs are known as 'man's best friend'.

Dogs are devoted to their human companions, and ask hardly anything in return. However, we can apply small changes to their daily routine to make our pups a little happier. Giving our pets extra treats, like biscuits, for example, could become an unhealthy habit. Instead, we could create some food puzzles that provide self-entertainment for our pups. **38**

Another way to keep our canine friends happy and avoid boredom is to organise 'play dates' at the park. Most dogs love to socialise, usually with other dogs, but also with humans. Arrange with other dog owners a time and a place where your pets can meet and play, even for just 15 minutes. Alternatively, you can take your dog to get some human attention at a pet-friendly café, for example. **39** It is important for a dog to understand that, after a period of rest, a time for physical activity will follow.

By observing our pets' behaviour, we can learn about their personalities and preferences. However, there are still some myths that many people believe to be true. For example, you might have heard that big dogs are more aggressive than small ones, but that isn't true. **40** Another misconception is that it is normal for dogs to have bad breath. In actual fact, having constantly bad breath could be a sign of teeth or gum problems. If that's the case, you should consider taking your dog to the vet for a check-up. **41** Although they can't see as many colours as we can, dogs are able to see a limited range of colours.

A fact about dogs that nobody can deny is the importance of their role in our past and present society. Years ago, dogs were especially useful around the farm to protect and herd sheep and cows. They were also helpful during hunting trips, by tracking and catching prey without eating it. **42** Those generally called 'police dogs' are taught to detect and find illegal items in public places. Others have the difficult task of finding and rescuing people in dangerous situations. Let's not forget the guide dogs, who help blind people lead a better life, or the dogs who provide company to elderly or lonely people.

Not everyone is a dog lover, but there's always something to learn from a dog. The dedication and love they show sets an example for many of us.

A   It is also (wrongly) believed that dogs can only see black and white.

B   Watching how our four-legged friends figure out how to feed themselves stimulates their minds, and it would be great fun for us too!

C   Some may argue that having a cat as a pet is better than having a dog, because they are not as needy and human-dependent.

D   Whatever activity you plan for your pet, you should establish a daily routine.

E   Nowadays, depending on their type of breed, dogs are trained in different ways to support humans in their jobs.

F   Dogs live in the present, enjoying every moment of their day.

G   Each dog has their unique personality that isn't affected by their size.

You are going to read a newspaper article about the differences between a book and a film. For questions 43–52, read the text below and, in the separate answer sheet, choose the correct paragraph (A–D).

Ready Player One
The book is always better than the film – is it true?

A This film is a definite must if you are a fan of '80s pop culture, but you can still enjoy it even if you don't know anything about that wonderful decade. Having read the book and watched the movie, I spotted many differences right from the start. The first part of the novel describes the setting in detail, but it doesn't feel slow or heavy. The movie, on the other hand, starts with action scenes that keep you glued to the screen for a while.

Despite this striking difference, the plot follows the exact same storyline as the book. The story is set in the not-so-distant future, where people spend as much time as possible in a virtual world called the Oasis, trying to escape their depressing everyday life. Before his death, the creator of this fantasy world designs some sort of treasure hunt by hiding clues across the Oasis. The player who follows the clues and finds the three keys inherits the creator's fortune and becomes extremely rich.

B The downside of reading a book set in such a specific and iconic period in time is that every reference has to be described in detail. If you are passionate about the '80s, you might find such a lengthy and precise description fascinating and amusing. If not, you might find yourself skipping whole paragraphs to get straight to the story. In contrast, the film's director doesn't need to talk the viewer through the '80s references. They are just visual clues shown in the right place at the right time for those who can recognise them, but they are not necessary for the film to be understood. In this respect, I feel that the movie can appeal to a larger audience than the novel.

C While spending their time in the Oasis, people can be anyone they want to be, as their real identities are hidden. Just as in a video game, the players choose a nickname and their own avatar. This fantasy world offers many arenas in which players can join in at any time in order to earn virtual money that can be spent as they wish.

That's where the main character, also known as Parzival, meets Art3mis – a cool girl with excellent fighting skills. It's love at first sight for this young man who spends more time in virtual reality than in the real world. But Art3mis keeps the two worlds clearly separate in her mind and knows that their relationship isn't real. She reminds him that they don't know each other and what they see is pure imagination. Making such an important point, as is so relevant nowadays, it is a shame that the film doesn't develop the topic further.

D The main difference between the book and the film is the description of the quest to find the clues. In the novel, Parzival spends most of his time trying to figure out the clues and find the keys. There are a number of challenging and elaborate tasks that the character has to perform and he does this on his own. In the film, however, the challenges are less complicated and a lot easier than in the book. Throughout his quest, Parzival can always count on the help of his friends and Art3mis.

I can't honestly decide whether the book is better than the film, but I can encourage you to give both a try and see if you can decide for yourself which one is better.

In which paragraph:

does the writer think that the film is better than the book?   43 [ ]

is life in the Oasis described?   44 [ ]

does the story appear simpler in the movie than in the book?   45 [ ]

does the writer suggest that the film can be good for everyone?   46 [ ]

does the writer express disappointment?   47 [ ]

is it suggested that the novel might be boring for some readers?   48 [ ]

does the writer tell the main point of the story?   49 [ ]

does the main character rely on his team to complete his mission?   50 [ ]

are the '80s references described as unimportant for the development of the plot?   51 [ ]

is the writer unable to express his preference between the book and the film?   52 [ ]

Answer sheet: Cambridge B2 First Reading

Test No. ☐

Mark out of 23 ☐

Name _____   Date _____

Part 5   *6 marks*

Mark the appropriate answer (A, B, C or D).

| 0 | A ▭ | B ▭ | C ▬ | D ▭ | |

31	A ▭	B ▭	C ▭	D ▭			34	A ▭	B ▭	C ▭	D ▭	
32	A ▭	B ▭	C ▭	D ▭			35	A ▭	B ▭	C ▭	D ▭	
33	A ▭	B ▭	C ▭	D ▭			36	A ▭	B ▭	C ▭	D ▭	

Part 6   *7 marks*

Add the appropriate answer (A–G).

| 37 | | 38 | | 39 | |
| 40 | | 41 | | 42 | |

Part 7   *10 marks*

Add the appropriate answer (A, B, C or D).

| 43 | | 44 | | 45 | | 46 | | 47 | |
| 48 | | 49 | | 50 | | 51 | | 52 | |

PROSPERITY EDUCATION
www.prosperityeducation.net

Cambridge B2 First
Reading: Parts 5–7

Test 3

You are going to read an extract from a novel in which a teacher describes a difficult time in her career. For questions 31–36, read the text and decide which answer fits best according to the text. In the separate answer sheet, mark the appropriate answer (A, B, C or D).

It was five minutes before the lesson and I couldn't gather the courage to walk into the classroom. I could hear their excited voices from the other side of the wall and I knew from their loud conversation that it was going to be a long day. It was almost the end of the academic year and all the students were looking forward to their holiday break. The whole year had been really difficult for me, a new Physics teacher. I had obtained my teaching qualification the previous year and this was my first teaching role. Although I was well prepared in the subject and I had a lot of patience, I knew nothing about managing adolescents. At that age, they should be treated like adults, even though they often act like children. You can't have a mature conversation with people who dance on their desks and move furniture around the classroom.

That class had always been wild and disrespectful, but on that Friday, they were especially unmanageable. When I finally entered the room, the students started throwing paper balls at me. They took me by surprise and I couldn't make them stop. They realised the situation had gone too far only when I ran out of the room in tears. I went to the bathroom and I cried for a

Line 15   while. It felt like hours, but, after a few minutes, I was out of there. The embarrassment of what had just happened was too much for me to go back to class, but I wasn't going to accept their behaviour! I looked at myself in the mirror and I washed my face. I couldn't let them win and I couldn't let them think that I was a coward. I wanted to show them that I was stronger than that.

I took a deep breath and I went back in with a big smile on my face. They were shocked to see me back. I started the conversation with a cheerful: "Sorry about leaving the room in such a rush! I wasn't prepared for such a warm welcome!" At that point, the students didn't know how to react. Taking advantage of their surprise, I started teaching as planned. I had made a huge effort to prepare an interesting lesson, and I ensured that every single student was involved in the activities. Although on the outside I appeared to be calm and confident, inside I felt quite different. Unexpectedly, the lesson carried on smoothly until the end. The students seemed genuinely happy to participate and to complete their tasks. At the end of the day, I left school with a strong feeling that something might have changed for the better.

On the following Monday, I couldn't wait to go back to my students. I was curious to see if their behaviour had changed after Friday or not. I was still nervous, but this time I had a good feeling about it all. Once again, I stood outside the door. I could still hear their voices, but the conversation wasn't as loud as it had been before. As I walked in, the students greeted me with a cheerful "Good morning, Miss!" and I couldn't believe my eyes! All the students were sitting obediently at their desks and their books were ready to be opened. I thought they were trying to trick me and I couldn't relax throughout the entire lesson. I was expecting all students to rebel against me at some point, but that never happened. I was immensely relieved.

The following days went by without a single incident. I became more relaxed and the students enjoyed my lessons more and more. They had been studying hard and I was pleased to see some improvement in their grades. On the last day of the term, I was getting ready to leave the classroom after the sound of the bell. The students hadn't left yet; they were still there, in the classroom, looking at me. For a moment, I thought they might have waited until the last day of school to attack me. Instead, they gave me a diary. They had filled it with pictures taken during their breaks and each student had written a kind note for me. One read "I have learnt a lot in your classes". This was amazing! Another student wrote: "I won't forget what you've done for us". I cannot express how I felt in that moment, but I knew then that I had done something good.

31   In the first paragraph, how does the teacher feel?

  A   Excited about the school holidays.

  B   Tired after a long school year.

  C   Nervous about facing the students.

  D   Bored of waiting outside the classroom.

32   Which students does the teacher work with?

  A   Teenagers

  B   Adults

  C   Young children

  D   Elderly people

33   What does 'it' refer to in line 15?

  A   The room full of students.

  B   The time spent in the classroom.

  C   The time spent washing her face.

  D   The time spent crying in the bathroom.

34   In paragraph 3, what does the teacher expect?

  A   To have problems at some point during the lesson.

  B   A warm welcome from her students.

  C   A different behaviour from the students.

  D   Students to work hard in class.

35   In paragraph 4, how does the teacher feel about going to class on Monday?

  A   Nervous and worried, as she was on Friday.

  B   Hopeful to see an improvement in the students' behaviour.

  C   Scared of the students' behaviour.

  D   Excited about seeing the students.

36   Why do the students give the diary to their teacher?

  A   To show the pictures they took in school.

  B   To say goodbye at the end of the year.

  C   To say 'thank you' and to show appreciation.

  D   To show their language improvement.

You are going to read a newspaper article in which the writer talks about people who live a very long life. Six sentences have been removed. For questions 37–42, read the text and choose from options A–G the sentence that fits each gap. There is one extra sentence that you do not need to use.

The Secret to Longevity

You might have a longer life if you live in the 'Blue Zones'

Generally speaking, since the early 1900s people's life expectancies have extended to an average of 70 years, having doubled across the globe in a century. 37 [ ] It is believed that there are several factors that can determine our lifespan. Daily habits, such as diet, physical exercise and our relationships with others have a much stronger impact on our lives than genetics. This theory has many supporters who believe that living in the 'Blue Zones' might considerably extend the duration of our lives.

The non-scientific term 'Blue Zone' refers to specific geographical areas across the globe, in which inhabitants tend to live much longer lives than anywhere else and have fewer chances of suffering from chronic diseases than anybody else. 38 [ ] The warmer climate is another aspect that these special areas share. Although there might be some Blue Zones yet to be discovered, some are very well known.

The Greek island of Icaria is considered to be one of these Blue Zones. Its inhabitants eat a diet based on fish, olive oil and home-grown vegetables. Hard physical work is performed every day, which keeps their bodies fit and healthy. Similarly, the Nicoya Peninsula in Costa Rica is home to some of the oldest people in the world. 39 [ ] There, they eat a plant-based diet and keep the consumptions of proteins to the minimum.

On the Italian island of Sardinia live the oldest men in the world. Like the inhabitants of Icaria, a large number of Sardinians are farmers and are used to physical work. They too have a healthy diet based on fresh fish and vegetables. 40 [ ] Their diet is soy-based and they practise a form of meditative martial art called Tai Chi. The last known Blue Zone is in Loma Linda, California, where a vegetarian community is held together by a strong bond of faith and friendship.

It is clear that healthy food habits play a key role in longevity. All the communities living in the Blue Zones share a similar kind of low-protein diet, based mainly on fruit and vegetables. 41 [ ] In the Blue Zones people don't choose to keep active by going to the gym. Their 'exercise routine' is built into their daily life, from farming and fishing jobs, to walking long distances to gardening.

To preserve their psychological wellbeing, each member of these communities usually finds their unique purpose in life. Supporting each other as a community gives a strong sense of belonging that keeps their morale strong and their spirits high. Last but not least, one of the key factors that contribute to longevity is how many hours people dedicate to sleeping. 42 [ ]

In a nutshell, the goal of a long life is achievable if we make small changes to our current lifestyles. Perhaps we should consider eating more vegetables and less meat while introducing more physical activities in our everyday life? Also, let's not forget to sleep as much as we need and to enjoy spending time with friends and family.

A   On the other hand, the oldest women in the world live on the Japanese island of Okinawa.

B   In addition to an average of eight hours' rest per night, it is common practice to have a short nap, known as a 'siesta', in the daytime, usually after lunch.

C   Despite this increase, the inequality of life's duration between countries is very large.

D   Another common feature of their lifestyle is physical work.

E   Interestingly, even though they live in different parts of the world, these remarkable people have many things in common regarding their lifestyle.

F   Society is expected to live longer because of better health care and improved living standards.

G   Their secret to a long life is keeping active by performing physical jobs until they reach an old age.

You are going to read a newspaper article about a modern taxi company. For questions 43–52, read the text below and, in the separate answer sheet, choose the correct paragraph (A–D).

Uber
The revolution of the taxi industry

A Uber Technologies Inc., better known as Uber, is a ride-sharing company that matches passengers with cars, operating through a website or a mobile application. From its origin in San Francisco, USA, Uber has spread globally and now operates across hundreds of different, densely populated urban centres worldwide. To order a ride, passengers can log on to the app, which informs them of the price of the service. When there is a high demand for rides, and in particularly busy areas or at extremely busy times, the fare might increase. In situations where trains have been cancelled, many passengers at railway stations might be looking for an alternative way to get to their destinations. Some of them choose to book an Uber ride. In similar circumstances, the cost of the service would be higher than usual. However, passengers travelling in the same direction could share the vehicle and the cost, making the fee more affordable.

B The company was founded in 2009 by two billionaire businessmen. The concept behind this ride-hailing service was born on New Year's Eve, when one of the two founders and his friends spent several hundreds of dollars hiring a private driver. However, the cost of direct transportation could be reduced if shared among passengers. From this experience, a new taxi service began to take shape. In its early years, the Uber app only allowed users to order luxury vehicles and was more expensive than a regular taxi service. A few years later, a cheaper version of the service was developed. This option, called UberX, is what truly transformed the taxi business. Uber drivers can use their own cars and must have a driver's licence and a smartphone or a tablet. They must also meet specific health and age requirements. In addition, the drivers must pass a background check, to protect passengers from potential dangers. In most countries where Uber operates, the cars must also pass yearly checks.

C Uber offers various options to accommodate all types of passengers. For example, rides with additional assistance are provided to elderly passengers or to those with physical disabilities. Cars with extra legroom are available, offering a very comfortable travel experience. A unique service has been designed that allows patients to get to and from their appointments with doctors, nurses and other health practitioners. The company has diversified its services depending on the geographical area in which it operates. In California, for instance, Spanish-speaking drivers are available, while, in specific US cities, an electric bicycle rental system has been put in place. The company, however, hasn't limited itself to transporting people. Nowadays, the range of services offered by Uber Technologies Inc. has expanded considerably, from taxis to food delivery. Recently, Uber has launched a service that matches temporary workers with suitable jobs and potential employers.

D The growth of new technologies and a rise in mobile communication have inspired others to follow Uber in the ride-hailing business. Several rival companies have popped up all over the world, offering their own 'unique' transport solutions. One of Uber's main competitors is Ola Cabs. Based in India, this is one of the fastest-growing businesses in the sector. They offer the option of renting cars by the hour or ordering a taxi ride in advance, allowing passengers to pay digitally or by cash if they prefer. Another company, Lyft, might threaten Uber's success and popularity with its taxi service. Lyft cars are easily recognised thanks to the pink moustaches placed on the front of each vehicle. Via is different from Uber, as it provides a taxi service at a more localised level. Passengers hoping to reach different destinations within the same area have the opportunity to share a Via car. This solution reduces the costs for the users, while maximising the earnings for the drivers.

Which paragraph:

gives reasons for the increase in the number of ride-sharing companies? | **43** |

illustrates Uber's ambition to develop in other sectors? | **44** |

mentions the types of areas in which Uber operates? | **45** |

talks about Uber's rivals? | **46** |

mentions the Uber service that shaped the ride-hailing business sector? | **47** |

informs about a service that can be an advantage for a specific group of professionals? | **48** |

gives a description of how the booking system works? | **49** |

implies that passengers' safety is important for the company? | **50** |

provides an example in which the taxi fare might be affected by the number of potential passengers? | **51** |

explains the first service offered by Uber? | **52** |

Answer sheet: Cambridge B2 First Reading

Test No. ☐

Mark out of 23 ☐

Name _____   Date _____

Part 5

6 marks

Mark the appropriate answer (A, B, C or D).

| 0 | A | B | **C** | D | |

31	A	B	C	D	
32	A	B	C	D	
33	A	B	C	D	

34	A	B	C	D	
35	A	B	C	D	
36	A	B	C	D	

Part 6

7 marks

Add the appropriate answer (A–G).

| 37 | | 38 | | 39 | |
| 40 | | 41 | | 42 | |

Part 7

10 marks

Add the appropriate answer (A, B, C or D).

| 43 | | 44 | | 45 | | 46 | | 47 | |
| 48 | | 49 | | 50 | | 51 | | 52 | |

Cambridge B2 First
Reading: Parts 5–7

Test 4

You are going to read an extract from a novel in which a man called Tom talks about his life after university. For questions 31–36, read the text and decide which answer fits best according to the text. In the separate answer sheet, mark the appropriate answer (A, B, C or D).

At the age of 22, my family life was far from ideal. I was just a child when my parents split up, but that wasn't the issue. Soon after their break up, my mum left our home to move abroad and I was left with my father, who looked after me to the best of his ability. The cause of my family problems was my father's relationship with someone who eventually became his second wife. I never really liked the woman, but I didn't know why. Although her behaviour was still considered acceptable, I felt extremely uncomfortable around her. Because of this, I began to imagine how life would be if I didn't live with them.

As I've mentioned, I was just a child and my everyday life was similar to those of the other kids'. I went to school and I did my homework every day. I also attended swimming lessons three times a week and had play dates with my classmates every Saturday afternoon. I didn't spend much time at home and I was busy enough not to worry about my step-mother. I managed to finish school with high grades, then I went to the other side of the country to attend university. I was too involved in my own life as a teenager first, then as a young man to care about what was happening at home. I would visit my father's house just during my holidays and they seemed happy together.

Line 17   Immediately after I graduated from university, I was offered an excellent job in my hometown. I wasn't thrilled at the idea of starting my new life there, but this opportunity was too good to miss. I excitedly started looking for my own place to rent, but I was shocked to see how expensive it was. Luckily, my father insisted that I should move back in with them. To be honest, the thought of sharing a confined space with my father and, even worse, with my step-mum wasn't appealing, but I had no choice, considering my limited finances. Another advantage to living at my dad's house was the location, which was ten minutes' walk from my new workplace. I didn't have to commute by bus or car, so I could save time and money.

My new job might not have been glamorous, but I was proud of the position I had been given and the company I worked for. I had been hired by one of the biggest retailers in the fashion industry as a supervisor in one of their many shops across the country. Not only was I leading a team of people who respected me, but I was also admired by my superiors for my problem-solving approach. I had finally found a place where I belonged and where I was free to express my opinions. Unlike most people, going to work was a pleasure for me, not a chore. I used to wake up before my alarm and spend a long time getting ready because I wanted to look as professional as I felt. My passion for retail and my dedication to the job allowed me to be the best employee I could ever be. Just over a year later, I was promoted to assistant manager and I was over the Moon by this achievement.

Despite my successful career, life at home had become increasingly difficult. My step-mother made it clear that I wasn't welcome in their house. In her view, they had let me move back in as a favour, and I was constantly reminded of this. My father was not aware of the way she was treating me, and I didn't want him to worry about it. Most importantly, I didn't want to put him in a position where he had to choose between his wife and his son. I had been trying to figure out a solution to this problem for months, but I had no luck. When my company advertised the launch of their new stores abroad, I saw it as a sign of destiny calling. I applied for a store manager position and after a long recruiting process I was offered the job. I couldn't believe my ears when they told me I had been selected to run a shop in Spain! All I had to do was to go home, pack my bags and tell my dad that I was leaving.

31   What is the main point of the first paragraph?

    A   To describe Tom's relationship with his father.

    B   To explain the origin of Tom's issues.

    C   To explain Tom's relationship with his step-mother.

    D   To talk about the difficulties of living alone.

32   How does Tom describe his childhood years?

    A   Very lonely

    B   Too busy

    C   Unusual

    D   Ordinary

33   What does 'there' refer to, in line 17?

    A   To the place where Tom comes from.

    B   To the house where Tom's dad and his wife live.

    C   To Tom's workplace.

    D   To Tom's university.

34   In the third paragraph, how does Tom feel about living in his family home?

    A   He is happy to live with his dad again, even if his step-mum is there.

    B   He is not happy to live there, but he can't afford to live by himself.

    C   He is excited about his new life there.

    D   He is grateful for his daily walk into work.

35   In the fourth paragraph, Tom enjoys going to work because:

    A   he has been given a promotion.

    B   he doesn't have to commute.

    C   he is appreciated for who he is.

    D   he is passionate about the fashion industry.

36   In the fifth paragraph, Tom's father:

    A   thinks that his son should move out.

    B   has to make a difficult choice about his wife.

    C   is worried because his son wants to move out.

    D   doesn't know about the problems between his wife and his son.

You are going to read a newspaper article in which the writer talks about the issues of work-related stress. Six sentences have been removed. For questions 37–42, read the text and choose from options A–G the sentence that fits each gap. There is one extra sentence that you do not need to use.

Burnout

Causes of work-related stress and how to deal with them

The term 'burnout' doesn't raise any positive feelings. Although it isn't a medical diagnosis, burnout describes a sense of physical and mental exhaustion, often caused by very long periods of stress. It often affects people who are responsible for others in their daily jobs. Over-achievers and perfectionists are more likely to be affected by burnout. **37** Achieving results that are 'just fine' but not 'perfect' is perceived as a failure, which causes unnecessary stress.

While a high-stress job doesn't automatically lead to burnout, it is important to assess whether you are at risk or not. As it is often difficult to establish when 'a lot' has become 'too much', regularly disconnecting from work and reconnecting with yourself is vital. **38** However, if you feel constantly exhausted and going to work becomes a real struggle, you might be suffering from burnout.

You should also consider any dramatic mood or behavioural changes. **39** An individual with a calm and patient personality who is finding it difficult to deal with others and struggling in performing regular work-related tasks might be on the verge of burnout. Often, unexplained headaches or stomach problems might be indicators of unmanageable stress levels.

Becoming aware of the causes of burnout is just as important as understanding the physical and psychological symptoms of the issue. **40** Occasionally experiencing time pressure or working over-time once in a while might actually have a positive impact on our productivity. However, working in an environment that pushes employees to the extreme, in terms of time, effort and dedication, can have devastating effects on their health.

Other aspects that might contribute to burnout are a lack of support from superiors and lack of clarity in the job role and its tasks. Preventing and dealing with burnout is a process that falls both on the employer and the employee. **41** Team-building activities and training sessions could be a solution to low morale and lack of engagement with work. On the other hand, employees should take the first step towards their own wellbeing. **42** When work seems to take over your life, make an effort to build social connections with co-workers, friends and family.

Last but not least, you should really make time for a hobby and some physical exercise. If you missed the signs and you are now dealing with it, look around you and find what makes you feel good. The goal here is to find your happy self again.

A   Weekends and holiday breaks usually give us enough time to rest, ready to start a new week with plenty of energy.

B   Requesting a meeting with their manager to express concerns regarding their psychological health could be a good place to start.

C   If you have always been passionate about your job, but you have now lost all interest in your profession, you should consider what might be the cause of this.

D   On the one hand, the employer should actively promote a work environment that supports and guides employees on a regular basis.

E   These types of people tend to set unrealistic goals for themselves.

F   Some experts believe that burnout isn't caused by work-related stress, but it is the result of other mental issues.

G   These are often combinations of several factors, such as unachievable targets, tight deadlines and unmanageable workload.

You are going to read a newspaper article about what to see in London as a family with children. For questions 43–52, read the text below and, in the separate answer sheet, choose the correct paragraph (A–D).

Visiting London as a Family
How to have a successful trip to London with small children

A   Visiting a city with very young children can be challenging and might easily become a stressful experience. To avoid any inconvenience, it is necessary to plan in advance. First of all, make a rough programme of what you want to see and when. Allowing enough time to visit your places of interest is key to a successful trip – and don't forget to include in your timetable the travelling time between destinations. You could involve your children in the planning stage by showing them pictures and videos of places they are going to see. Another aspect to consider is how you will be getting around the city centre. In London, the underground trains (also known as 'the tube') and buses are cheap and readily accessible, although having a pushchair or a buggy might cause a bit of a struggle. Luckily, most Londoners are willing and happy to help, even if they don't often smile!

B   London is served by six airports. Heathrow, Gatwick and City airport are the most central, making the journey into the central areas of London less time-consuming. From any of these airports, you can easily get to the accommodation of your choice by underground train. The other three airports, Stansted, Luton and Southend, are further away from London, but are very popular for their low-cost flights. From these airports, you can't get on the Tube, but the train service into London is frequent throughout the day and coaches run almost 24 hours a day. My personal favourite is Stansted airport. Despite being an extremely busy airport, its terminal isn't as big as the one in Heathrow or Gatwick. Another advantage is that it is conveniently located between London and Cambridge.

C   There is plenty to see and do in London for adults and children of all ages. Without a doubt, your kids will love spending a few hours at Hamley's, which is believed to be the largest toy store in the world. On each of its seven floors there is plenty to see, do and buy. For a stress-free visit, you and your children should agree on a small budget they are allowed to spend, before entering the shop. If you are trying to keep the costs of your trip to a minimum, you can't miss the Natural History Museum and the Science Museum, where there are plenty of interactive displays and activities for children of all ages. Although there is no entrance fee, a small donation is always welcomed. Seeing a musical in London is a unique experience and you can find many theatres that offer shows suitable for children. You might need to book in advance to find cheaper tickets.

D   If you want to make the most of your trip, I would suggest visiting places of interest for grown-ups when the children are taking their afternoon naps. If you are a fan of museums, in London you'll be spoiled for choice, depending on your interests. My favourite museum is the British Museum – its collection of Egyptian mummies is famous worldwide. The Sea Life Aquarium and London Zoo are fantastic places if you are an animal lover, but the tickets are quite expensive when visiting as a family. A ride on the London Eye delivers a breath-taking view of the whole city of London. If this is your first visit, you might want to avoid Madame Tussauds waxwork museum. Taking pictures with life-like wax statues might sound entertaining, but it is quite expensive and it is not that exciting. There is so much more to see in London!

Which paragraph:

lists several ways of getting into the city?

| 43 | |

describes what adults should visit when children are sleeping?

| 44 | |

gives advice on what to do before the trip?

| 45 | |

warns about a place that seems a waste of time?

| 46 | |

talks about how you can get to London from Stansted?

| 47 | |

mentions different ways of reaching destinations within the city?

| 48 | |

describes museums with child-friendly entertainment?

| 49 | |

suggests giving children the chance to manage their own money?

| 50 | |

talks about an attraction that offers wonderful scenery?

| 51 | |

suggests cheap deals when landing far from the city?

| 52 | |

Answer sheet: Cambridge B2 First Reading

Test No. [　　]

Mark out of 23 [　　]

Name _____ Date _____

Part 5

6 marks

Mark the appropriate answer (A, B, C or D).

| 0 | A | B | C■ | D |

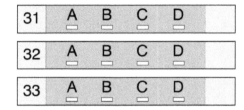

31	A	B	C	D
32	A	B	C	D
33	A	B	C	D

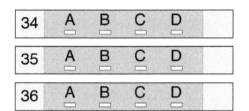

34	A	B	C	D
35	A	B	C	D
36	A	B	C	D

Part 6

7 marks

Add the appropriate answer (A–G).

| 37 | 38 | 39 |
| 40 | 41 | 42 |

Part 7

10 marks

Add the appropriate answer (A, B, C or D).

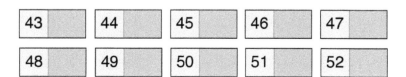

| 43 | 44 | 45 | 46 | 47 |
| 48 | 49 | 50 | 51 | 52 |

PROSPERITY EDUCATION
www.prosperityeducation.net

Cambridge B2 First
Reading: Parts 5–7

Test 5

You are going to read an extract from a biography in which the writer talks about her passion for flying. For questions 31–36, read the text and decide which answer fits best according to the text. In the separate answer sheet, mark the appropriate answer (A, B, C or D).

Line 2

I remember walking on the beach as a child, holding my mum's hand and comparing the shades of blue of the sky and the sea. I loved them both, as they gave me a feeling of freedom. Despite my young age, I was a confident swimmer. Splashing around in the waves, I felt free and in control. There was something safe about swimming in the sea. In contrast, I felt small and powerless when looking at the immense sky. We lived near an airport and I enjoyed watching the planes fly by right above our heads, and my mum would encourage me to say hello to the pilots. "Wave your hands!" she used to say. "Look, they are waving back at you!" I very much doubt that she could see the pilots from such distance but, even now, I like to think that it was true. What a fascinating machine, so big and heavy, yet able to lift itself off the ground and move across the sky. I wondered how it would feel to work in an airplane, taking passengers from one country to another.

As the years went by, my passion for planes and flying never faded away. Life had several surprises in store for me, and I had many ups and downs, but the biggest surprise was yet to come. I was living and working away from my family and friends, in an unfriendly town. I had been there a year, but I still couldn't settle – even worse, I felt trapped. In my constant search for freedom and personal satisfaction, I kept surfing the web for a job that would take me away from that hostile place and would give me a better chance in life. Just when I had almost given up, I came across a job advert that changed my life forever.

It was a mid-week, boring afternoon at work and my eyes were glued to my computer screen while reading about a low-cost airline hiring cabin crewmembers. I quickly applied for the position, but then I forced myself to forget about it. What if they didn't reply? I didn't have to wait long to find out that I had been invited to attend an interview. They were meeting job candidates in several locations across Europe, so I had to organise a little trip abroad. I took some days off work, but I couldn't tell anybody the real reason I was going to be away, in case I didn't get the job. I carefully planned my journey there and back. I booked a cheap room in a hostel and I prepared possible answers for my interview – and then the interview was intense and lasted several hours. After talking to all the candidates, the airline representatives announced who had been selected for the position. I was in! It was impossible to contain my joy and I remember calling friends and family back at home to let them know the good news.

When I resigned from my job at that time, my boss tried to convince me to stay. Unfortunately for him, I had a brand-new future waiting for me. I left that unwelcoming town and moved abroad, to a town near the airport that was going to be my base. I had to attend a month-long training course, but I was still excited about the idea of spending my days in the sky. The course wasn't in my native tongue and that was very challenging. Despite the difficulties, my motivation pushed me to study hard and pass my exam at the end of the training. The excitement of flying everyday was something I had never experienced before. Some of the other flight attendants didn't enjoy spending hours inside an airplane, but I felt as free as a bird.

I didn't get to stay abroad overnight and I didn't get to visit exciting places because we operated only short-haul flights across Europe, but I wasn't bothered. Spending my days in the air and going back home every night gave the right balance of excitement and stability to my life. Waking up at 3am for the early shift wasn't easy, however, but it was a small price to pay for the joy of flying. It was just a job, but it changed my life. I met people who became close friends and I settled in a country where I've always felt at ease, just like a home away from home.

31   What does 'them' refer to, in line 2?

    A   The beach and the writer's mum.

    B   The writer's mother and father.

    C   The sea and the sky.

    D   The beach and the waves.

32   In the first paragraph, airplanes are appealing to the writer because:

    A   they can travel from one country to another.

    B   they can fly over the sea and across the sky.

    C   they are big and can carry many people.

    D   they can fly high despite their weight.

33   In the second paragraph, what is the most unexpected life event the writer talks about?

    A   Living in an unwelcoming town without family or friends.

    B   Finding a vacancy as a flight attendant.

    C   Getting the job of her dreams.

    D   Settling in a new place after living there for a year.

34   In the third paragraph, why does the writer call her family and friends?

    A   To tell them she had been given the job.

    B   To inform them that the trip had gone well.

    C   To have a chat after a long and tiring day.

    D   To ask for help in planning her trip abroad.

35   In paragraph 4, why is the training course difficult for the writer?

    A   It is longer than expected.

    B   There is a difficult exam at the end.

    C   It is in a foreign language.

    D   There is too much to study.

36   In the fifth paragraph, this job has transformed the writer's life because:

    A   she has to wake up very early in the morning.

    B   she has the opportunity to travel to other countries.

    C   she always returns to her house after work.

    D   she is comfortable in a foreign land.

You are going to read a newspaper article in which the benefits and drawbacks of attending a university are analysed. Six sentences have been removed. For questions 37–42, read the text and choose from options A–G the sentence that fits each gap. There is one extra sentence that you do not need to use.

Studying Abroad

The good, the bad and the ugly about studying in another country

Before the daily chores and responsibilities of adult life kick in, studying abroad can be a golden opportunity for young men and women. 37[ ] Given the appeal of such an adventure, it is therefore not surprising that the number of students applying to foreign universities has increased throughout the years. For college students, the advantages of attending an academic programme abroad can be endless, but there can also be some negative aspects that might be useful to be aware of.

One of the obvious reasons for students to attend a university abroad is the opportunity to live a different way of life from what they are used to and to see museums, landmarks and natural wonders of the hosting country. 38[ ] If studying in France, for instance, it would be easy enough to visit nearby countries such as Spain, Germany or Italy. Of course, education is what drives students to make this decision in the first place. By enrolling in a 'study abroad' program, the student will be immersed in a different style of education, which might take some time to get used to.

After completing their course of study abroad, students will have gained academic knowledge of course, but they will have also achieved a wider range of skills than they would studying in their home country. When returning home, students often find that they have better chances at getting their dream job than those who attended university in their home country. 39[ ]

Living abroad often implies learning or improving a foreign language. This is especially true when education is the main purpose for the move. Studying abroad allows you to completely immerse yourself in the language of your host country, not only in an academic setting but also in a social environment. Whether you are reserved and shy or a social butterfly, you shouldn't miss out on discovering new interests and taking part in new activities that you wouldn't find in your country. One of the main benefits of being a student abroad is the large number of interesting people you might meet, some of whom may become lifelong friends.

40[ ] There is no doubt that it can be extremely exciting and engaging; however, some students might experience different levels of culture shock. It is believed that people go through a few culture-shock phases. In the first phase, the students are filled with excitement for the new adventures ahead. 41[ ] At this point, it is important to talk about these differences while trying to understand them. Finally, the period of acclimatising usually begins. There is no rule to when it might start and how long it may last, but this is when the student begins to accept unfamiliar aspects of their new lifestyle.

People living abroad, who feel disoriented and unsettled while experiencing a new way of life, experience this phenomenon. 42[ ] Universities often offer help to tackle this unpleasant period. In the meantime, students can combat culture shock by setting a daily routine that suits their needs, adopting a healthy lifestyle and keeping in contact with family and friends back at home.

A   Furthermore, this temporary move abroad allows the student to visit neighbouring countries.

B   Perhaps the most intriguing and possibly challenging aspect of living abroad for a student is the chance to experience, first-hand, different food, culture and traditions from their own.

C   It gives them the chance to explore another country and experience a new culture while laying the foundations for their future.

D   It is not understood why some students might enjoy this experience more than others.

E   This positive period is followed by one of frustration, in which differences between the home country and the host country are discovered and experienced.

F   Feeling lonely and homesick, losing sleep and lacking confidence are common symptoms of culture shock.

G   Employers are often attracted by potential employees who have such a valuable life experience.

You are going to read a newspaper article about the origins of tea and coffee. For questions 43–52, read the text below and, in the separate answer sheet, choose the correct paragraph (A–D).

Coffee and Tea: Fascinating Drinks
There is always a good reason for a cup of coffee or tea

A A hot coffee in the morning, for an energy boost, and a cup of tea in the afternoon, for a catch-up with a friend. There are many reasons to enjoy a 'cuppa', with coffee and tea being the most popular hot drinks worldwide. The origin of the coffee bean is uncertain, dating back probably earlier than the 15th century in Ethiopia. However, the interest in drinking coffee quickly spread from Yemen to the rest of the Middle East, South India and northern Africa. It then spread to Europe, Southeast Asia and America. The history of tea originates in around the 3rd century, in Southwest China, where it was drunk as a medicinal beverage and later on as refreshment. This drink spread to other East Asian countries and then to Europe.

B The legend of the first cup of coffee in the world tells about an Ethiopian farmer, who felt energised and revitalised after eating certain berries. He took the red berries to a monk, who wasn't impressed and threw them into the fire. The pleasant aroma attracted other monks, who removed the toasted beans from the fire, turned them into fine powder and mixed it with hot water. A legendary Chinese account of the origin of tea involves a poor farmer who decided to improve the conditions of a temple he saw every day on his way to his fields. He didn't have the funds to do any work to the temple, so twice a month for several months, he cleaned it up and burnt incense as an offering to the goddess Kuan Yin. She appeared in one of his dreams and, once he had woken up, the farmer did as he was told to do in the dream. He found a small tea plant in a cave under the temple. He took it home, replanted it and watered it until the small plant became a bush. After sharing some cuttings with his neighbours, the farmer started to sell the plant across the region.

C What's more intriguing than its legends is the culture of preparing and serving a hot cup of tea. Special ceremonies have developed in China and Japan, where specific rituals are applied when offering tea to refined guests. In the United Kingdom, the majority of the population drinks tea daily. This drink is consumed at home or in cafés, or tearooms, where it is often enjoyed with pastries or a slice of cake. In the Middle East, most cultures see tea as a vital part of their cuisine. Pouring is one of the techniques involved in serving tea. When poured from elevated heights, the flavour, texture and temperature of the tea are positively affected. Although in some European countries tea is served with a slice of lemon, milk is the most common addition to this drink.

D Researchers have discovered that drinking tea regularly several times a week can improve consumers' general health. Containing antioxidants, tea might help keep our bodies young for longer and could protect us from the damages caused by pollution. It is believed that not only does tea lower blood pressure, but it can also prevent teeth and heart problems. Tea contains a much lower percentage of caffeine than coffee, which can be dangerous for our nervous system if consumed in large quantities. Despite these possible downsides, drinking coffee also has some advantages. Similar to tea, coffee might contribute positively to our physical health. What's more, drinking coffee seems to have a positive effect on people's behaviour and mental abilities. Coffee appears to encourage participation in group activities and promote a positive view of self and others. Regardless of your drink of choice, both coffee and tea can be good for our health if consumed in moderation.

Which paragraph:

mentions a drink that brings advantages to our psychological health?   **43** [ ]

talks about small fruit with invigorating and exciting properties?   **44** [ ]

describes a way of improving the taste of tea?   **45** [ ]

talks about the country where coffee comes from?   **46** [ ]

informs the reader about the amount of a specific natural substance found in coffee and tea?   **47** [ ]

talks about a countryman who was repaid for his hard work?   **48** [ ]

indicates two Asian countries that show similarities in their tea culture?   **49** [ ]

explains the reasons for drinking tea in ancient times?   **50** [ ]

mentions a part of the world where tea is a fundamental part of the diet?   **51** [ ]

lists the effects that coffee and tea can have on our bodies?   **52** [ ]

Answer sheet: Cambridge B2 First Reading

Test No. ☐

Mark out of 23 ☐

Name _____   Date _____

Part 5   *6 marks*

Mark the appropriate answer (A, B, C or D).

0	A	B	**C**	D	

31	A	B	C	D			34	A	B	C	D	
32	A	B	C	D			35	A	B	C	D	
33	A	B	C	D			36	A	B	C	D	

Part 6   *7 marks*

Add the appropriate answer (A–G).

37		38		39	
40		41		42	

Part 7   *10 marks*

Add the appropriate answer (A, B, C or D).

43		44		45		46		47	
48		49		50		51		52	

PROSPERITY EDUCATION
www.prosperityeducation.net

Cambridge B2 First
Reading: Parts 5–7

Test 6

You are going to read an extract from a novel in which the writer describes his experience in the countryside. For questions 31–36, read the text and decide which answer fits best according to the text. In the separate answer sheet, mark the appropriate answer (A, B, C or D).

We were slowly climbing a steep path on the mountains. On our left, there were only rocks. On our right, there was a fascinating but dangerous waterfall – I definitely didn't want to fall down there! In the distance, we could see trees and beautiful green fields. The sky was blue and the birds were singing; what a wonderful day for an outdoor experience. It was quite chilly as the Sun was still rising, but the cool air gave me energy and made me feel refreshed. As we walked, we were getting increasingly hungry. We found a suitable spot for a quick picnic, then we carried on walking. We started off walking as a group, but we gradually split up. My dad was ahead, followed by my uncle, John, who kept talking continuously about his old friend Simon. He was impressed by my dad's speedy pace and his youthful energy despite his age. I could see my father speeding up, probably to impress my uncle even more or to
Line 11   distance himself from him.

In the group behind them, my aunt Beth, my mum and my sister kept a steady, leisurely pace, while chatting about clothes, recipes and something else that I didn't find interesting enough to listen to. I was in the last group with my cousin Jill. We were now going through the woods: the strong smell of mushrooms and moss was around us. Both Jill and myself felt happy and safe there. We wanted to sit on a fallen tree and chat all day, but we couldn't stop. We knew had to reach our destination before the Sun was high in the sky. It's funny how time seems to pass quickly or slowly depending on who you are with or what you are doing. Well, when I was with my cousin, time always passed incredibly quickly.

It wasn't long before we reached the end of the woods. The trees were behind us and there was an immense field, more beautiful than I had imagined. My uncle's country villa was there, right before our eyes. The others had already got in, opened the windows and started a fire. I went into every room, looking for something to do, but there weren't any jobs left for me to do, so I tried to make myself useful by getting involved in the kitchen, but my aunt and Jill didn't need any help. They cooked a fabulous lunch, after which we all went for an afternoon nap. We woke up refreshed and cheerful. We were all in a good mood, happy to chat by the fire, when my uncle made an announcement. He wanted to read us a letter that he had received not long before our trip to the countryside.

The letter was from one of his old friends, Simon, who, when he told my uncle about his health issues, was immediately invited to his country cottage, just like my uncle had done with us! In the letter, Simon expressed his gratitude for the generous invitation, but he hadn't expected to be there by himself. My uncle had left the cottage the day before as he had to go back to work urgently. Simon was worried about getting bored in the countryside, without TV and an internet connection. He was also concerned about the possibility of any kind of emergency that might occur. He wasn't sure how he would survive for a whole weekend in such a remote place, away from society. Luckily, Simon felt in perfectly good health during his stay at the cottage and enjoyed exploring the surrounding area. He spent his days there swimming in the lake and sunbathing on the grass.

After listening to my uncle read the letter, we had a light snack and we went to bed very early. I must have been exhausted, as I fell asleep immediately. We woke up early and it was freezing. We got dressed and went outside to find some wood for the fire. Unfortunately, the wood was damp and we couldn't light the fire to keep us warm. We couldn't even make a coffee! My uncle gave each of us a wetsuit and a large clean towel. When we were ready, he took us to the lake, just behind the trees. "There's no better way to get warm than a little swim!" he said. We stared at him in shock. Being February, the water temperature must have been below zero degrees Celsius! Nevertheless, we didn't want to upset him, so we quickly jumped in the lake and swam vigorously for a few minutes. He was right: we didn't feel as cold once we were out of the water!

31   In the first paragraph, how does the writer feel during his walk?

   A   He is worried about the dangerous path they are walking on.

   B   He feels tired from the long and difficult walk up the mountain.

   C   He is surprised about how fast everyone is walking.

   D   He feels happy to be on this country walk.

32   Who does 'himself' refer to, in line 11?

   A   The writer's father

   B   Uncle John

   C   The writer

   D   The uncle's friend

33   In paragraph 2, how does the writer feel about spending time with his cousin?

   A   He enjoys her company and would like to spend more time talking with her.

   B   He feels that they have been talking for too long.

   C   He would like to stay in the woods because he doesn't want to listen to her.

   D   He is happy to spend time with her but would like to walk faster.

34   In the third paragraph, what does the writer do when he arrives at the country villa?

   A   He helps his aunt and cousin cook lunch for everyone.

   B   He can't find anything to keep himself busy.

   C   He gets the house ready for everybody's arrival.

   D   He goes to explore the surrounding area.

35   In paragraph four, how does Simon feel about spending the weekend alone in the countryside?

   A   He is grateful for the opportunity to have some peace and quiet.

   B   He is worried about damaging the house.

   C   He is nervous about being isolated.

   D   He is happy to be away from technology.

36   In the fifth paragraph, they are all shocked because:

   A   there is no fire for their morning coffee.

   B   there is no heating in the house and it Is really cold.

   C   Uncle John suggests swimming in the freezing lake.

   D   Uncle John is upset when they all jump in the lake.

You are going to read a newspaper article in which the writer talks about her experience as an English teacher in China. Six sentences have been removed. For questions 37–42, read the text and choose from options A–G the sentence that fits each gap. There is one extra sentence that you do not need to use.

My Chinese Experience

China can be the destination of your dreams as an English teacher

Whether you are experienced and need a change or a newly qualified English teacher looking to gain experience, you should definitely consider working in China. You might start by committing to a six-month contract, but then end up staying for a few years, just like I did! **37**☐ Since the '70s, foreign visitors and workers have been allowed into the country, and with the lifting of the one-child policy, the English-teaching industry has boomed. In addition, social and economic globalisation are the main reasons for great demand of teachers of English as a foreign language across China.

If the charm of discovering a new way of life and experiencing a different culture is what is attractive to you about moving to China, rest assured you won't be disappointed. However, keep in mind that different locations will offer very different lifestyles. As you might expect, due to its cosmopolitan nature, living in a city might be a better option if you worry about culture shock and if you want to limit your chances of standing out. Cities offer a wide range of ways to spend your time, from museums to parks and gardens. **38**☐ Another advantage of living in a city is that you'll be spoiled for choice with a huge number of language schools to choose from.

39☐ Expect to be fully immersed in the traditional life and to meet locals. This is a very unique experience that wouldn't be as intense if you lived in a large city. You'll be truly treated as a celebrity, so don't be surprised if locals want to take pictures of you or even of your shopping trolley! The downside to this is that everyone knows who you are, but the advantage is that you'll get an insight of the Chinese life unlike anyone else would.

Whether you choose to live in a city or in a village, you'll find that Chinese people are friendly and warm-hearted. **40**☐ Don't be shy and accept their kind invitations to immerse yourself in their culture. They will feel honoured to have you as a part of their life, while you'll be gaining invaluable, life-long memories.

If the prospect of earning and saving money is your main reason for moving to China, know that you could potentially save around 40–50% of your salary. Using your common sense is key here. **41**☐ Some schools might offer you free accommodation, while others might pay for your return flights! Once you're there, learn to eat and shop like a local, avoiding tourist shops and Western restaurants. **42**☐ Travelling across and out of the country is relatively cheap, so make the most of your time abroad to visit as much as you can.

A   If you want to take a break from the delicious local cuisine, you can find plenty of Western restaurants, like pizzerias and fast food chains, which will give you a taste of home.

B   You'll soon notice that Chinese customs and traditions are very different from your own and it might take you a while to get used to them.

C   As teachers are well-respected figures in society, you can expect to receive presents and be invited to dinners and parties.

D   Although making money might be your goal, take advantage of this great adventure and explore!

E   The level of English in China is generally low, but the need to confidently communicate in this foreign language has increased, due to internal and external factors.

F   First of all, carefully select the school you want to work for and negotiate your salary before you move.

G   On the other hand, if you choose to start your Oriental experience in a village, be prepared to be the star of the show.

You are going to read a newspaper article about party entertainers. For questions 43–52, read the text below and, in the separate answer sheet, choose the correct paragraph (A–D).

Live Entertainment for Hire
Find the right performance for an unforgettable event

A   Are you planning a relaxed corporate event, an unusual wedding reception or a wild birthday party? Whatever the event, the Singing Waiters will deliver the perfect performance to suit your needs. Silver Service is a group of enthusiastic and talented singers who will spice up your event, getting your guests to dance and sing along! The Singing Waiters start by joining the staff, perhaps serving food or drinks. This will give them the chance to assess the audience and to build rapport with the guests. After a few hours of this 'undercover mission', and when the time is right, the singing waiters will begin their 30-minute performance. As the songs will have been chosen in advance by you, there's no room for disappointment. The outstanding singing skills of the 'waiters' will make sure that your guests have a wonderful time and their impeccable timing will add a surprise element to your party.

B   If you are looking for an explosive performance, look no further. The Diva Decades is the only tribute act of its kind, transporting you through the years of music, from the 60s with Tina Turner's rock'n'roll to the 80s with Madonna and Cher, finishing off with Jesse J and Beyoncé for the younger audience. The three singers combine vocal talent, themed costumes and cool dance routines to create a party to remember. The Diva Decades will deliver an outstanding performance at your private party or corporate event, but only across Scotland, as they are based in Glasgow. The group was formed in 2016 by a singer and choreographer who hoped to put together an energetic, all-female act that was at the same time fun and professional. Their shows can last as long as 90 minutes, with a 15-minute break halfway through.

C   FUSE is a duo of gifted artists who play pop, club and crossover tracks with their electric violins, each worth over one million dollars. The instruments are made of a heat-resistant, strong synthetic fibre and are sprayed with a paint that incorporates gold particles. Each violin is decorated with over fifty thousand Swarovski crystals, which have been individually applied. What's more impressive than these beautiful musical instruments is FUSE's ability to transform well-known tracks into something truly amazing, as their skills are, without a doubt, extraordinary. Linzi Stoppard has been playing the violin since the age of four, before attending prestigious music schools where she also mastered clarinet and piano. Similarly, Ben Lee started playing the violin when he was five years old. As a teenager, Ben won several awards and, in 2013, for the fifth time, became the fastest violin player in the world. With such a unique style, it doesn't come as a surprise that FUSE have played with stars of the music scene and performed at Royal events.

D   Gem O'Reilly can cater for any kind of event as a professional solo singer, guitar player and songwriter. Depending on your preference, this wonderful artist can sing and play covers or her original songs, or a combination of both. During her almost two-and-a-half-hour performance, Gem covers a range of genres such as pop, rock, country, soul, folk and acoustic. Her career started at the age of 17, when Gem was signed to an American record label. Her first original album reached number 7 in the iTunes Chart. In 2014 and 2019 her second and third albums were released, showing Gem's impressive progression in the music industry. Her gigs vary from live bars to weddings, to corporate events. This artist has performed at many prestigious venues in the UK. Although she is based in London, Gem is happy to travel all over the country to bring her lovely melodies to your event.

Which paragraph:

talks about artists who started playing musical instruments since a very young age?

| 43 | |

describes an act that is willing to perform anywhere in the country?

| 44 | |

mentions a singing and dancing performance?

| 45 | |

illustrates an act that needs to spend time with the guests before the performance begins?

| 46 | |

doesn't mention the duration of the performance?

| 47 | |

tells about a group formed by women only?

| 48 | |

describes extremely expensive musical instruments?

| 49 | |

talks about a multi-talented artist?

| 50 | |

mentions events in which the artists shock the guests with an unexpected performance?

| 51 | |

describes a cover group that combines different elements to deliver a unique performance?

| 52 | |

Answer sheet: Cambridge B2 First Reading

Test No. [ ]

Mark out of 23 [ ]

Name _____

Date _____

Part 5

6 marks

Mark the appropriate answer (A, B, C or D).

0	A	B	C ▬	D

31	A	B	C	D		34	A	B	C	D
32	A	B	C	D		35	A	B	C	D
33	A	B	C	D		36	A	B	C	D

Part 6

7 marks

Add the appropriate answer (A–G).

37		38		39	
40		41		42	

Part 7

10 marks

Add the appropriate answer (A, B, C or D).

43		44		45		46		47	
48		49		50		51		52	

PROSPERITY EDUCATION
www.prosperityeducation.net

Cambridge B2 First
Reading: Parts 5–7

Test 7

You are going to read an extract from a novel in which the writer talks about her experience as a contestant on a TV game show. For questions 31–36, read the text and decide which answer fits best according to the text. In the separate answer sheet, mark the appropriate answer (A, B, C or D).

Like every Tuesday evening at 8.30, most people were glued to their TV screens this week, watching a famous game show. It had gained popularity due to its simple format and the unique selection process its contestants go through, one for each region of the country. The show had been advertised for months before being aired live on a regular basis. The TV studio was small and it couldn't contain a large audience, but that increased its appeal. In the middle of the studio the host was standing by a colourful desk while I was sitting on his left-hand side and my opponent, Darius, on his right-hand side. I was one of the two finalists and the chance of winning a life-changing one million pounds was very close. It was difficult to keep calm and hide the hundreds of thoughts going through my mind. I started biting my nails and suddenly the stool I was sitting on felt incredibly uncomfortable. Darius, on the other hand, appeared calm and collected, and I found his bright smile and confident hand gestures extremely distracting.

The show host was wearing a tailor-made suit, no doubt expensive, and was covered in fake tan and makeup. He reminded me more of a robot than a real person, with his scripted lines and well-practised movements, all planned in advance by the production team. I gladly welcomed a short break while the advertisement was being shown. I remembered why I had put myself literally on that seat. My ultimate dream was to make a new life by the sea for my husband and me. Oh how I missed the feeling of sand between my toes and the smell of the sea air! I never wished for fancy villas and luxury cars, but I did wish for a slower pace of life
Line 20   and a peaceful lifestyle – we both did. The advert break gave me the chance to drink some water and control my breathing, but we were soon back live on the show.

As the camera light went on, there was a short introduction from the host and then it was time for the last question, which separated me from the prize money. It was my opponent's turn to answer first and he still seemed relaxed, while I could hear my own heartbeats. The host read out the question, loud and clear: "Who was the only legitimate son of King Henry VIII?" For the first time, Darius looked confused and his hands were shaking. I was shocked to see how quickly he had lost his confidence. He kept staring at the five options on his screen with a worried look on his face. When the time was about to run out, he randomly picked one of the options and it was clear that he was just trying to guess. I couldn't believe it, but he had chosen the wrong answer, and it was my turn now. The host repeated the question for me. I gave my answer as quickly as I could "Edward VI, crowned at the age of 9 and died at the age of 15!" As soon as the host announced it was the correct answer, he shook my hand and my husband, who was sitting in the crowd, ran to the centre of the studio to celebrate with me.

The programme was shown a few weeks later and everyone in my village recognised me. They were curious to know about the show and what happened behind the scenes, but after a while I got bored with all the questions. Nevertheless, I always made time to answer them because I still enjoyed being the centre of attention. At the same time, the locals thought that I was a very polite person! At the end of the day, it had been a fantastic experience all-round and they loved hearing about it. As soon as my winnings reached my bank account, my husband and I took our first steps towards our new life. We quit our jobs and moved abroad to buy a little house on the beach that I had always wanted. We have been leading a simple life since then, growing our own vegetables and looking after our chickens. Our lives changed completely since that day when I won one million pounds.

31   In the first paragraph, how does the writer feel?

     A   She is calm and relaxed.

     B   She is worried but confident.

     C   She is happy and cheerful.

     D   She is nervous and agitated.

32   In the second paragraph, why does the writer compare the host to a robot?

     A   Because the host is wearing a lot of makeup and expensive clothes.

     B   Because of the way the host was moving around the studio.

     C   Because the host was speaking and moving very slowly.

     D   Because the host's general behaviour wasn't spontaneous and seemed unnatural.

33   Who does 'both' refer to, in line 20?

     A   The writer and her husband.

     B   The writer and her opponent.

     C   The writer and the host.

     D   The host and Darius.

34   In the third paragraph, why does Darius change his behaviour?

     A   Because he doesn't want to lose the money.

     B   Because he doesn't know the correct answer.

     C   Because he knows the correct answer.

     D   Because he's running out of time.

35   In paragraph four, why does the writer answer all the questions?

     A   Because she is bored and she enjoys chatting with the locals.

     B   Because she doesn't want to be considered rude by the locals.

     C   Because she loves being famous.

     D   Because the locals love hearing about the TV show.

36   In the fourth paragraph, the writer's life-long dream is to:

     A   resign from her position and live in another country.

     B   have a farm and grow fruit and vegetables.

     C   live by the seaside.

     D   have a big house and expensive cars.

You are going to read a newspaper article in which the writer discusses the advantages and disadvantages that social media brings to modern society. Six sentences have been removed. For questions 37–42, read the text and choose from options A–G the sentence that fits each gap. There is one extra sentence that you do not need to use.

The Pros and Cons of Social Media

Social media has improved global networking, but it comes at a cost

Since the early 2000s, the phenomenon of social media has grown at an extremely fast pace. As the number of households and institutions that rely on technology increases, so does the number of social media users worldwide. Unsurprisingly, just like any other tool, online networking platforms have brought many advantages to our modern society as well as disadvantages.

The purpose of social media is to connect people far and wide. The main advantage of social platforms is their level of connectivity: it's the fastest, most reliable and most accessible way to get in contact with anyone in the world. **37** Regardless of background and location, online networking facilitates learning and teaching. Other positive effects of sharing and receiving information across the globe are the raising of awareness regarding important social issues and the opportunity to solve and prevent crime.

Among the benefits brought to our society by social media, there is also a whole new range of jobs, from content writer to influencer. With an ever-growing audience, social platforms are the ideal space to advertise all sorts of products and services. **38** This is really a win-win situation for companies that can reach a wide audience while keeping the costs down, and for influencers, who get paid to advertise, and for the viewers, who can often choose whether to watch the advert or skip it, and whether to virtually 'follow' an influencer or not.

39 As anyone can create a personal account on any online platform without any checks, nobody knows who is hiding behind the screen. This can seriously affect children and teenagers, who spend hours on social media.

40 This is most common among young social-platform users. This mean behaviour is often displayed anonymously, so the bully doesn't have to confront the victims face-to-face. The impact of these types of attacks is devastating and can bring long-lasting negative effects to their victims. For the protection of all social media users, laws have been put in place, allowing cybercriminals to be prosecuted. **41** It's never a good idea to respond to an online bully, but saving evidence of the upsetting messages can be useful.

Together with online bullying, scams and frauds are another disadvantage of social media, due to the lack of privacy concerning personal information that is out there. This kind of cybercrime can be carried out from any location in the world and can affect not only those who aren't technology experts, but also those individuals who are tech-savvy. **42**

It is believed that a prolonged use of social media could lead to real-life social isolation or to health issues due to the lack of physical exercise. However, despite these potential risks, there is no doubt that social media has enhanced global connectivity.

A   There is a wide variety of online, dishonest schemes and the criminals behind the screens are often technologically skilled.

B   Similarly, sharing opinions, information, knowledge and experience has become easier, which has allowed for tremendous advances in education.

C   On the other hand, if used incorrectly, social media can have a negative impact on our everyday lives.

D   With that in mind, many companies rely on influencers' videos to promote their brands.

E   Although it is difficult to find out who is committing the offence, victims should find the courage to speak up and seek help.

F   Most users access their online accounts from mobile devices, such as smartphones and tablets, but social media started with desktop computers.

G   Cyberbullying is the use of technology to embarrass or threaten others through messages, photos or videos posted online.

You are going to read a newspaper article about the four types of communication. For questions 43–52, read the text below and, in the separate answer sheet, choose the correct paragraph (A–D).

The Art of Communicating

Mastering the four types of communication can improve your personal and professional life

A Verbal communication, whether by speaking or using sign language, is the most common way to share information with others. As this type of communication is efficient and immediate, and has a high impact on our audience, it is important to develop it as we would do with any other skill. When talking to a group of people, like when delivering a presentation for example, a confident and clear voice is necessary. A strong voice attracts people's attention and inspires authority. It is equally important that the information shared is presented logically and simply, so that it can reach as many individuals in the audience as possible. Although they might seem helpful while gathering your thoughts, filler words, such as 'like', 'uhm', 'yeah', should be avoided as listeners find them distracting. As communication involves sending and receiving information, if you want to be a good communicator, you should also improve your listening abilities.

B It is believed that 55% of communication is nonverbal, including body language, gestures and facial expressions. Nonverbal communication can be intentional – when you smile while greeting a customer at work for example – or unintentional, like crossing your arms when feeling uncomfortable. It is important that we train ourselves to control our body language, ensuring that our verbal and nonverbal communication convey the same meaning, so as to avoid sending contrasting messages. A simple exercise can be repeated throughout the day, as we experience a range of emotions (happiness, anger, boredom). By identifying how our emotions manifest themselves in our bodies, it should become easier to control our body language and change it if required. Do we clench our fists when angry? Focus on opening and relaxing your hands. Do we curve our backs when bored? Straighten your shoulders and hold your head up high.

C By written communication we mean the act of writing, typing or printing symbols, such as letters and numbers, to share information. Traditionally, we do this through books, pamphlets, magazines, letters and notes; however, it seems that, in recent years, the use of written communication has increased, through emails, texts messages and chats. Unlike any other type of communication, this provides a record of the message conveyed. The downside of written communication is that we can't rely on tone (jokes, excitement, disappointment) and visual clues to convey the full meaning. For this reason, it is a good idea to express our thoughts as clearly and as simply as possible to avoid any misunderstandings. If you want to appear professional and competent, double check your writing to spot any mistakes you might have made. If you have the chance, ask someone you trust to check it too. If writing to others is one of your frequent tasks, it might be worth keeping a file of sample writings that you find useful.

D Visual communication is often used to support other types of communication and can be very effective when chosen and used correctly. Photographs are great tools to explain a point you want to make, but each photograph needs a purpose. Adding pictures just to fill up the slides would simply distract your audience. Drawings and diagrams can be useful when photographs aren't suitable or available. However, drawings need to be at a very high standard and diagrams need to be precise if you want to give your presentation a professional finish. Graphs, maps and tables are ideal for presenting data, but they might become confusing if they are too detailed or contain too much information. Bringing actual objects to demonstrate how something works, for example, will grab your audience's attention throughout your presentation. If the object is too large, it can be successfully replaced by a model. Nowadays, videos are frequently used in presentations, but limiting the length of the videos is key to keep your listeners engaged.

Which paragraph:

gives examples of communicating through physical movements?	**43**
describes the possibility of tracking communication as a unique feature?	**44**
talks about a type of communication that is mainly used to assist the other types?	**45**
mentions a skill that should be developed in order to advance one type of communication?	**46**
describes the type of communication that technology has affected the most?	**47**
illustrates a type of communication that can be spontaneous or controlled?	**48**
mentions a type of communication that needs a variety of items to convey meaning?	**49**
discourages the use of specific words?	**50**
warns the reader about opposite meanings within the same message?	**51**
suggests that someone else should check the message before it is shared?	**52**

Answer sheet: Cambridge B2 First Reading

Test No. ☐

Mark out of 23 ☐

Name _____   Date _____

Part 5   6 marks

Mark the appropriate answer (A, B, C or D).

| 0 | A ☐ | B ☐ | C ■ | D ☐ | |

31	A ☐	B ☐	C ☐	D ☐	
32	A ☐	B ☐	C ☐	D ☐	
33	A ☐	B ☐	C ☐	D ☐	

34	A ☐	B ☐	C ☐	D ☐	
35	A ☐	B ☐	C ☐	D ☐	
36	A ☐	B ☐	C ☐	D ☐	

Part 6   7 marks

Add the appropriate answer (A–G).

| 37 | | 38 | | 39 | |
| 40 | | 41 | | 42 | |

Part 7   10 marks

Add the appropriate answer (A, B, C or D).

| 43 | | 44 | | 45 | | 46 | | 47 | |
| 48 | | 49 | | 50 | | 51 | | 52 | |

PROSPERITY EDUCATION
www.prosperityeducation.net

Cambridge B2 First
Reading: Parts 5–7

Test 8

You are going to read an extract from a novel in which the writer describes a stressful shopping experience. For questions 31–36, read the text and decide which answer fits best according to the text. In the separate answer sheet, mark the appropriate answer (A, B, C or D).

Prior to the COVID-19 pandemic of 2020, my monthly trips to the supermarket had always been the source of jokes between my husband and I, as he would say something like "Has my wife got carried away again?" or "Are we feeding the whole town this month?" Without fail, I would always fill up about five or six large, re-usable carrier bags, to ensure we made it until the end of the month. I knew my husband was convinced that I always bought more than a household of two people needed, but I loved cooking and we both enjoyed eating well. In a way, however, I could see his point of view. I was used to buying as much as my fridge and kitchen cupboards could take. I grew up watching my mother doing the same, and her mother

Line 9 before her, so that's where I picked it up from. Perhaps because of these memories, there was something very calming and comforting about walking around the aisles, looking at new and unusual products while putting basic groceries in my basket.

While I found food shopping very relaxing, my husband didn't like crowded places, so he avoided supermarkets at all costs. It might sound unfair, but I was the one in charge of choosing what to eat for both of us – from packed lunches to dinners. To be honest, I wouldn't have wanted him by my side while filling up my trolley: he would have tried to hurry me, turning a usually pleasant experience into a stressful one.

For our peace of mind, we came up with a successful shopping routine. Every payday after work, I would make my way to the local supermarket where I would spend about 45 minutes to one hour doing the shopping. I would have plenty of time to get our day-to-day food and carefully select some treats for special evenings. I would send him a text just before approaching the till, and he would pick me up and put the shopping in the boot of our car. Once home, we would unpack our groceries together and store them properly. My husband always looked amazed at the amount of food I could fit in our regular-sized freezer!

We had promised ourselves that we weren't going to lose our minds despite the situation across the country. After all, my husband and I didn't need to panic because we had enough supplies to last us a couple of weeks. People in other countries were reacting to these difficult times in different ways: some were rushing to buy medicines, others were stocking up on cleaning products, while in our country, people were panic-buying their groceries. I struggled to find a reason for this, as all major supermarket chains had assured us that there would be plenty of food for everyone. Nevertheless, in these unusual circumstances, people were preparing for the unexpected and were buying twice or three times as much as they needed. Despite their best efforts, the supermarket workers weren't able to keep up with the demand and the shelves were mostly empty. My husband and I both worked full-time and it was impossible for us to just pop in the shop at any time of the day to find some vegetables and the other few bits we wanted. For this reason, we had to come up with a plan.

That Wednesday morning, we got up an hour and a half earlier than usual, at 5am. We grabbed a few carrier bags and drove to the biggest supermarket in the area. We were not prepared for what we saw. Despite the early hours and the shop still being shut, the length of the queue outside its doors was shocking. Everybody was quietly waiting for the doors to open and I could see the fear in some people's eyes. In an attempt to lighten the atmosphere, my husband tried to start a conversation with those waiting next to us. Despite the cold weather, he even managed to make a few people smile with his jokes. The supermarket finally opened to the public and we all entered calmly. I could see that some shelves hadn't been re-stocked. Just ten minutes later, people started behaving very differently, from running across the shop to verbally abusing the cashiers. Suddenly, the place in which I had always felt safe and comfortable turned into a very unsettling environment. I looked around as I became increasingly anxious. I grabbed a few vegetables and guided my husband to the tills because I simply couldn't stand that place anymore.

31　In paragraph 1, the husband says that his wife:

   A　spends too much money on shopping.

   B　doesn't have enough re-usable bags.

   C　buys too much food.

   D　often cooks for their neighbours.

32　What does 'it' refer to, in line 9?

   A　The food that the writer bought every month.

   B　The habit of buying large amounts of food.

   C　The memory of going shopping with her mother.

   D　The husband's opinion on shopping.

33　In the second paragraph, the writer feels:

   A　disappointed that she has to do the shopping by herself.

   B　upset that her husband doesn't like supermarkets.

   C　annoyed because she finds shopping stressful.

   D　glad that her husband isn't shopping with her.

34　In paragraph 3, how does the writer describe their shopping day?

   A　Well-organised and predictable.

   B　Stressful and chaotic.

   C　Expensive and time-consuming.

   D　Rushed and challenging.

35　In the fourth paragraph, the writer doesn't understand:

   A　how the supermarkets are preparing for difficult times.

   B　why people are buying so much more than usual.

   C　why supermarkets don't have enough supplies for everyone.

   D　how she could find the time to buy vegetables.

36　In paragraph 5, how does the husband behave outside the supermarket?

   A　He's chatty and cheerful.

   B　He's quiet and scared.

   C　He's tired and feels cold.

   D　He's annoyed because his wife wants to leave the shop.

You are going to read a newspaper article that describes how people's behavior changed during the spread of COVID-19. Six sentences have been removed. For questions 37–42, read the text and choose from options A–G the sentence that fits each gap. There is one extra sentence that you do not need to use.

Standing Together Against a Common Enemy

When a pandemic developed across the globe, people became generous and compassionate

Modern society has been frequently accused of being selfish and insensitive towards other people's needs and emotions. It is argued that it is necessary to put yourself first before helping others, but there's a fine line between self-preservation and selfishness. The peak of a lack of consideration for others became apparent at the beginning of 2020, when a new virus spread across the world with catastrophic consequences. When authorities worldwide confirmed it was a pandemic, panic kicked in.

For fear of food shortages, people crowded the supermarkets to stock up on essentials. **37** In addition, the measures taken to contain the spread of the 'coronavirus', such as 'social distancing' and self-isolation, increased the risks of death by loneliness. There was a real concern about the consequences of emotional isolation across the whole population, especially those in specific age groups or those who face daily physical and/or mental challenges.

While many announcements were made to reassure shoppers that stockpiling of food and other goods was unnecessary, supermarket staff worked hard at replenishing the shelves and ensuring the smooth running of the stores. **38** In addition, consumers unable to get to the supermarket due to health reasons were given priority on home-delivery slots. These thoughtful measures had two positive effects. Not only did they give everyone a fair chance of getting the vital items they needed, but it also protected the older population from contact with younger people, who stood a better chance of surviving the virus.

Despite some incidents of unkind and greedy actions, communities worldwide came together to help those in need. **39** Instinctively, fear can bring out the worst in people, which is why it is important to celebrate those who make an effort to put others first and to show that kindness can be beneficial for the global community.

With the help of technology and social media, it is easy to keep connected while keeping physical distance from oneanother. In the UK, a support group was created by a worker who found herself without a job due to the virus outbreak. This young woman decided to spend her free time helping others during those difficult times. She started by distributing leaflets through people's letterboxes in her area, offering to deliver food and medicines to those who needed it. Her group was set up on an online platform, in which volunteers were asked to participate. **40**

Other groups offered help to the families who were financially affected by the COVID-19 pandemic and were struggling. **41** That's where these support groups came into play, cooking healthy meals for those who had lost their jobs and who had suddenly found it difficult to provide for their families. **42** Yoga and fitness instructors uploaded videos to promote physical activity, while tourist guides, without any tourists around, shared their knowledge online, providing companionship to those stuck at home.

Although fear can have a strong impact on people's behaviour, it is during unsettling and uncertain times that mankind shows its ability to put differences aside and comes together against a common enemy.

A   Various types of voluntary groups spontaneously popped up all over the world to provide emotional and practical support, showing that generosity and compassion for others are strong features in mankind.

B   Not only groups but also many individuals got creative and took it upon themselves to help others in whichever way they could.

C   COVID-19, commonly known as 'coronavirus', is a new disease that spreads very quickly and can affect people's lungs and airways.

D   As the virus spreads quickly and easily among people, many countries ordered the closure of businesses that involve social gatherings to take place, such as bars, pubs and restaurants, causing many job losses.

E   In the meantime, to reduce the problems caused by panic-buyers, supermarket chains put aside their commercial rivalry and agreed on dedicating specific shopping hours to customers over 60, and to those who work in the emergency services.

F   Sadly, this irresponsible behaviour caused serious issues for vulnerable and elderly people, who weren't able to get the supplies they needed.

G   Surprisingly, the response was so great that this group expanded from the south of London to other parts of the country, as far away as Cornwall, Northern Ireland and Scotland.

You are going to read a newspaper article about measures taken to prevent the spread of the coronavirus. For questions 43–52, read the text below and, in the separate answer sheet, choose the correct paragraph (A–D).

Are You Doing Your Bit?

From individuals to governments, everyone has a role to play in this fight against the new pandemic

A As of March 2020, there was no vaccine for COVID-19, so it was necessary to avoid any exposure to the virus to prevent ourselves from becoming ill. The recommended basic protective measures for everyone to apply were easy to follow. One of the key words used from the beginning was 'hygiene': we should wash our hands as often as possible. In the UK, it was suggested that we use soap and water to wash our hands for as long as it takes to sing 'Happy Birthday' twice, about twenty seconds. This was especially important, the government told us, if we had been in public places and after coughing, sneezing or blowing our noses. When soap and water weren't available, a good alternative was to use hand sanitisers that contain at least 60% alcohol. Many people began to wear plastic gloves and face masks, hoping to further shield themselves from the virus. Unfortunately, this particular virus spreads very easily, so we were not to touch our faces. Habitual and common behaviours such as rubbing our eyes, biting our fingernails and picking our noses were also to be avoided as much as possible, especially if our hands hadn't been washed.

B Another key word associated with virus prevention is 'physical distancing'. Simply put, it is required to keep a two-metre distance from anyone who doesn't live in your household, especially if they are ill. In addition, whether we are showing symptoms of a disease or not, we should stay away from vulnerable people, such as the elderly and those with other serious health issues. Originally, the term used to describe the avoidance of physical contact was 'social distancing', but many people found it upsetting. The term in this case was, in fact, incorrect as no one and nothing was stopping us from keeping in touch with loved ones and society. However, we had to learn new ways to socialise. Thankfully, we live in an era of advanced technology that can provide an acceptable alternative to face-to-face communication.

C Of course, as well as protecting ourselves, we should also think about protecting others. Even if we aren't showing any signs of a disease like COVID-19, we should try to avoid crowded public places and reduce the contact we have with others – for example, working from home, if possible, and limiting the number of times we go out. At home and at work, we should clean and disinfect objects and surfaces that are touched or used frequently, such as keyboards, desks, light switches, tables and countertops. However, the measures are even stricter if we feel unwell. If the symptoms are mild, we can easily recover at home, but we should do our best to keep away from other household members and pets. We should stay in an allocated 'sick' room and wear a face mask if someone enters that room. This so-called 'home isolation' might be frustrating, but it's the best chance we have at avoiding passing on such a virus to the rest of our family and friends.

D As the pandemic affected every country, governments worldwide took a course of action to fight the spreading of the virus. Some countries applied stricter measures than others, but they all generally followed a similar pattern of procedures. The first step taken was prevention, to slow down the spread of the disease. That's where hygiene and physical distancing came into play. The second step was preparation for the disruption caused not only by the gradual closure of air, sea and land borders between countries, but also by the need for people to stay at home. A pandemic can have an impact on everyone's daily life, from public transport to social interaction, to work/study routines. For this reason, governments had to implement a plan that protected the physical, mental and economic wellbeing of all citizens.

Which paragraph:

explains that keeping our distance from others is necessary to protect older people from falling ill?

| **43** | |

illustrates the importance of good hygiene in a domestic and professional environment?

| **44** | |

describes how to keep fingers and palms clean?

| **45** | |

clarifies what countries have been doing to put a stop to this pandemic?

| **46** | |

suggests that electronic devices can help individuals maintain contact with financial stability of the population?

| **47** | |

mentions the importance of creating a scheme to defend the health and the financial stability of the population?

| **48** | |

suggests that people have to become flexible regarding how they connect with others?

| **49** | |

lists some day-to-day activities that might be affected by the virus?

| **50** | |

explains how infected people should behave?

| **51** | |

talks about items that might work as barriers against COVID-19?

| **52** | |

Answer sheet: Cambridge B2 First Reading

Test No. [ ]

Mark out of 23 [ ]

Name _____

Date _____

Part 5

6 marks

Mark the appropriate answer (A, B, C or D).

0	A	B	C	D	

31	A	B	C	D		34	A	B	C	D
32	A	B	C	D		35	A	B	C	D
33	A	B	C	D		36	A	B	C	D

Part 6

7 marks

Add the appropriate answer (A–G).

37		38		39	
40		41		42	

Part 7

10 marks

Add the appropriate answer (A, B, C or D).

43		44		45		46		47	
48		49		50		51		52	

Answers

Answers   Cambridge B2 First Reading   Test 1

Part 5		Key words from the questions	Clues from the text
31	C	...first paragraph...nervous / ...starting her own business	...first project as a wedding planner / ...leave her stable 9–5 job to pursue such a financially unpredictable career
32	B	In paragraph 2...announcement...Sunday / ...members...together	...knew they would have all been there at that time.
33	A	...third paragraph...family...doesn't support her dreams / ...Jade...traditional lifestyle	...family had never been supportive / ...they wished she had a conventional lifestyle.
34	C	...line 23...'played it safe' / careful, avoiding risks	... they had never pushed themselves out of their comfort zones. / They had never tried anything new in their life...
35	D	...fifth paragraph...call the bakery / ...location of the cake	...what had happened. / ...slowed down the traffic – the cake was on its way.
36	D	In paragraph 6...arrive, the guests / unhappy and confused	...atmosphere was tense / ...Some seemed shocked, some seemed upset, in contrast with the music.

Part 6		Key words from the questions	Clues from the text
37	F	...escape this fast-paced living...most of us...break...holiday...hobby...to reduce stress	...overwhelmed...everyday life / On the other hand...a small number of people...abandon modern society completely...
38	B	However, religious spiritual and moral beliefs are frequently the cause	Often, technology, stress and work overload...factors that contribute...
39	D	...have to work hard...roof over our heads and food on our tables	...basic human needs have to be met / ...choose to build their own house / ...feeding themselves...
40	G	The biggest obstacle...how to sustain it.	...financially challenging / ...finding creative ways to pay / ...work from home...
41	A	Many...funds and assets acquired before...solitude	...quite common...savings or state pensions...reclusive...
42	E	First of all...increases creativity...sharpens ...focus	...some advantages / In addition...physical and mental relaxation

Part 7		Key words from the questions	Clues from the text
43	A	...not suitable...quiet and private	...wrong place for a romantic...
44	C	...negative first impression...outside	...neon...sign above the door wasn't...appealing...cheap and cheerful...look.
45	B	...wasn't prepared...	...confident...would be ready...arrival. / Instead...wait almost an hour to be seated.
46	B	...slow service	...were really hungry / ...wait about 45 minutes to be served.
47	A	...uncomfortable and overcrowded	...incredibly busy / ...noise levels were so high / Extra tables were added...had to move my chair every time ...
48	D	...let down...former member	Manager...resigned and left / ...run away with my deposit money.
49	C	...positive, long-lasting impression	...fantastic...experience...won't forget!
50	C	...Asian food	...waiting staff...traditional oriental costumes.
51	D	...understanding...customer's issue	...very sympathetic...my situation. / ...didn't have to pay ...missing sum.
52	A	...average food	...a sign of good food. / Unfortunately, this wasn't the case. / ...meal wasn't bad...wasn't memorable / ...food was very basic ..portions...small

Answers   Cambridge B2 First Reading   Test 2

Part 5		Key words from the questions	Clues from the text
31	D	...first paragraph...main point / description...personality	I wasn't a sociable teenager / ...they...complete opposite of me / ...unlike me / I was happy to spend...
32	B	...second paragraph...option...choose / earn some money...summer job.	...making some money, instead of spending it, sounded like a much better alternative.
33	A	...paragraph 3...difficult...get a job / mature employees...experience...preferred.	...young age...lack of work experience...weren't what...looking for.
34	C	...fourth paragraph...feel...job offer / mixed feelings	...whether to laugh or cry. / What if... / On the other hand, I was excited...
35	B	...paragraph 5...arrives...realises / a part of a team	As soon as I got to the camp...introduced...other entertainers. / ...working with other staff members
36	B	...'them'...line 46 / Life experiences	...life experiences...going through

Part 6		Key words from the questions	Clues from the text
37	F	...live in the present...enjoy every moment	...don't care...don't think...or worry / For this reason ...appreciation for life.
38	B	...figure out...feed themselves...great fun for us too!	...food puzzles...self-entertainment
39	D	...activities...daily routine	...pets can meet and play. / ...pet friendly café. / ...after a period of...a time for...will follow.
40	G	...unique personality...isn't affected...size	Big dogs...more aggressive than small...isn't true.
41	A	...(wrongly) believed...only see black and white.	...can't see as many colours as us...limited range of colours.
42	E	trained in different ways...support humans...	...hunting trips / ... 'police dogs'

Part 7		Key words from the questions	Clues from the text
43	B	...think...film...better than the book	I feel...movie can appeal to a larger audience
44	C	...life in the Oasis...	...in the Oasis, people can be / ...fantasy world offers many arenas / ...earn virtual money
45	D	...story...simpler in the movie...	In the film, however, the challenges are less complicated and a lot easier...
46	A	...film...good...everyone...	...a definite must if / ...but you can still enjoy it even if
47	C	...disappointment	...it is a shame that the film doesn't
48	B	...novel...boring...some readers	...lengthy and precise description / ...skipping whole paragraphs
49	A	...main point...	...the plot ...storyline / The story is set...were people
50	D	...rely on his team...	...always count on the help of his friends and Art3mis.
51	B	...'80s references...unimportant for...the plot	...just visual clues / ...but they are not necessary for the film to be understood.
52	D	...unable...preference...	...I can't honestly decide whether the book is better than the film

Part 5		Key words from the questions	Clues from the text
31	C	first paragraph...does the teacher feel? / ...nervous...the students	...couldn't gather the courage to walk into the classroom / ...from their loud conversation it was going to be a long day / The whole year had been difficult ...
32	A	What students / teenagers	... adolescents / At that age, they should be treated like adults, even though they often act like children.
33	D	... 'it'...line 15 / time...crying...bathroom	...bathroom and I cried for a while. It felt like hours, but after a few minutes, I was out of there.
34	A	...paragraph 3...teacher expect / ...problems during lesson	Unexpectedly, the lesson carried on smoothly until the end.
35	B	...paragraph 4...teacher feel...going to class on Monday / hopeful...improvement...behaviour	...nervous but / ...had a good feeling about this.
36	C	why...give the diary / 'thank you' / appreciation	...kind note / "I have learnt a lot in your classes" / "I won't forget what you've done for us" / ...had done something good.

Part 6		Key words from the questions	Clues from the text
37	C	Despite this increase...life's duration...countries	...extended / ...doubled across the globe / ...lifespan
38	E	different parts of the world...these remarkable people...things in common...lifestyle	...specific geographical areas across the globe / ...inhabitants / ...live much longer / ...fewer chances of suffering ... / ...than anybody else.
39	G	Their secret to a long life...keeping active...physical jobs	...hard physical work / Similarly / ...oldest people in the world
40	A	On the other hand...oldest women...Japanese island	...oldest men in the world / ...soy-based / ...meditative martial art
41	D	Another common feature...physical work	...share a similar kind of ... / ...don't choose to keep active by going to the gym / 'exercise routine'...farming...fishing jobs...walking long distances...gardening
42	B	eight hours' rest per night...short nap, known as a 'siesta'	...hours / ...sleeping

Part 7		Key words from the questions	Clues from the text
43	D	...reasons...increase...companies	...new technologies / ...mobile communication / ...inspired others / Several companies have popped up...
44	C	...ambition...other sectors	...hasn't limited itself / ...has expanded considerably, from taxi to food delivery / ...matches temporary workers with suitable jobs and potential employers.
45	A	...types of areas...operates	...now operating across hundreds of different densely populated urban centres worldwide.
46	D	...rivals	...main competitors / ...might threaten Uber's success and popularity
47	B	...service...shaped...sector	...is what truly transformed the taxi business.
48	C	...advantage...specific group of professionals	...unique service / ...health patients to get to and from their appointments with doctors, nurses and other health practitioners.
49	A	...how...booking system works	To order a ride, passengers can log on to the app, which informs them of the price of the service.
50	B	...passengers' safety...important	...background check, to protect passengers from potential dangers.
51	A	...example...taxi fare...affected	...in particularly busy areas or at extremely busy times, the car fare might increase / In situations where trains have been cancelled / In similar circumstances, the cost of the service would be higher than usual.
52	B	...first service	...a new taxi service began to take shape. / ...its early years...

Answers   Cambridge B2 First Reading   Test 4

Part 5		Key words from the questions	Clues from the text
31	B	...main point...first paragraph / ...origin...issues	...but that wasn't the issue / The cause of my family problems was my father's relationship
32	D	...childhood years / ordinary	...my everyday life was similar to those of the other kids / I went to school and I did my homework... / ...swimming lessons...play dates
33	A	'there'...line 17 / ...comes from	...hometown / ...own place to rent
34	B	...third paragraph...living...family home / ...not happy...can't afford...by himself	...sharing...wasn't appealing / ...had no choice...limited finances
35	C	...fourth paragraph...enjoys work / appreciated	...people who respected me...admired / ...belonged...free to express my opinions
36	D	...fifth paragraph...father / ...doesn't know...problems	...was not aware...I didn't want him to worry...

Part 6		Key words from the questions	Clues from the text
37	E	These types of people...unrealistic goals	Over-achievers...perfectionists / ...results that are...not 'perfect'...failure
38	A	Weekend and holiday breaks...rest...plenty of energy	...regularly disconnecting from work...reconnecting to yourself / ...constantly exhausted / ...going to work...a real struggle
39	C	Passionate about your job, but...now lost any interest	...mood or behavioural changes / ...calm and patient personality who...difficult to deal
40	G	These...combination of several factors / ...unachievable targets, tight deadlines and unmanageable workload	Causes of the issue / ...time pressure...working over-time / ... in terms of time, effort and dedication
41	D	On the one hand, the employer should	...the employer and the employee / Team-building activities and training sessions / On the other hand, employees should
42	B	...their manager...their psychological health...a good place to start	Employees / ...first steps / ...their own wellbeing

Part 7		Key words from the questions	Clues from the text
43	B	...several ways...into the city	...making the journey into the central areas of London / ...the train service into London is frequent throughout the day and coaches run almost 24 hours a day
44	D	...adults visit...children are sleeping	...visiting places of interest for grown-ups when the children are taking their afternoon nap
45	A	...do before the trip	...plan in advance / ...make a rough programme / ...planning stage
46	D	...place...waste of time	...you might want to avoid / ...but it is quite expensive and it is not that exciting
47	B	...reaching your hotel	...can easily get to the accommodation of your choice
48	A	...different ways...reaching destinations...within the city	...getting around the city centre / the underground...the buses
49	C	...museums...child-friendly	...interactive displays and activities for children / ...offer shows suitable for children
50	C	...children...their own spending money	...you and your children should agree on a small budget they are allowed to spend
51	D	...attraction...wonderful scenery	...delivers a breath-taking view of the whole city
52	B	...cheap deals...landing...far from the city	...further from London / ...low-cost flights

Answers   Cambridge B2 First Reading   Test 5

Part 5		Key words from the questions	Clues from the text
31	C	...'them' / line 2 / sea...sky	The sky and the sea / ...they gave...freedom
32	D	...first paragraph...airplanes are appealing / ...fly high...despite/weight	...fascinating machine / ...big and heavy / ...yet able to lift itself off the ground / ...move across the sky
33	B	...unexpected life event...second paragraph / ...vacancy...flight crew member	...biggest surprise was yet to come / ...a job advert that changed my life forever
34	A	...call family and friends...third paragraph / ...given the job	...to let them know the good news
35	C	...training course difficult...fourth paragraph / ...foreign language	...wasn't in my native tongue and that was very challenging
36	D	...transformed life...fifth paragraph / ...comfortable...foreign land	...settled in a country / ...felt at ease / ...a home away from home

Part 6		Key words from the questions	Clues from the text
37	C	it...them...another country...new culture...foundation...future	...golden opportunity / ...young men and women / ...appeal of such adventure
38	A	Furthermore...neighbouring countries	...different way of live...and to see / ...France...Spain, Germany or Italy
39	G	employers...attracted...potential employees...valuable life experience	...chances / ...dream job / ...those who attended...
40	B	...intriguing...challenging...experience first-hand different food, culture and traditions from their own.	...exciting and engaging / ...however...
41	E	This positive period...followed by one of frustration/differences...are discovered and experienced.	...filled with excitement / ...these differences while...
42	F	...lonely and homesick, losing sleep and lacking confidence...symptoms	feel disoriented and unsettled / Universities often help...unpleasant period

Part 7		Key words from the questions	Clues from the text
43	D	...advantages...psychological health	...positive effect / ...behaviour and mental abilities
44	B	...small fruit...invigorating and exciting properties	...berries / ...energised and revitalised
45	C	...improving the taste of tea	...flavour / ...positively affected
46	A	...country...coffee comes from	...the origin of the coffee bean / Ethiopia
47	D	...amount of specific natural substance...coffee and tea	...tea contains a much lower percentage of caffeine than coffee.
48	B	...countryman...repaid...hard work	...farmer / ...improve the conditions of a temple / ...twice a month for several months, he cleaned it up and burnt incense as an offering to the goddess / ...started to sell the plant across the region
49	C	...two Asian countries...similarities...tea culture	China and Japan / ...special ceremonies / ...specific rituals
50	A	...reasons for drinking tea...ancient times	...3rd century / ...medicinal beverage and later on as a refreshment
51	C	...part of the world...tea...fundamental part of their diet	...Middle East / ...most cultures / ...vital part of their cuisine
52	D	...effects...coffee and tea/bodies	...lower blood pressure / ...prevent teeth and heart problems / ...Similar to tea, coffee might contribute to our physical health.

Part 5		Key words from the questions	Clues from the text
31	D	...first paragraph / ...happy...country walk	...fascinating...waterfall / ...beautiful green fields / ...what a wonderful day for an outdoor experience
32	A	...'himself'...line 11 / ...the writer's father	...my father
33	A	...paragraph 2...spending time with his cousin / ...enjoys her company...spend more time with her	...chat all day / ...with my cousin, time always went incredibly quickly.
34	B	...third paragraph...what does the writer do when he arrives / ...anything to keep himself busy	There weren't any jobs left for me to do / ...I tried to...but
35	C	...paragraph four...Simon...spending the weekend alone / ...nervous...isolated	Simon was worried about getting bored in the countryside / He was also concerned about the possibility of any kind of emergency
36	C	...fifth paragraph...shocked / ...swimming in the freezing lake	...a little swim / ...the water temperature must have been below zero degrees

Part 6		Key words from the questions	Clues from the text
37	E	The level...generally low...internal and external factors	...have been allowed into the country / ...the lifting of the one-child policy / In addition, social and economic globalisation are the main reasons / ...great demand of teachers of English...
38	A	...find plenty of Western restaurants...a taste of home	...culture shock... / Cities offer a wide range / Another advantage of living in a city...
39	G	On the other hand...experience in a village...star of the show	...traditional life and to meet locals / ...wouldn't be as intense if you lived in a large city / ...treated as a celebrity
40	C	...teachers are well-respected figures...be given presents and invited to dinners and parties.	...friendly and warm-hearted /...accept their invitations / ...feel honoured to have you
41	F	First of all...select the school...negotiate your salary	...save around 40–50% of your salary / Some schools might offer you...
42	D	making money...goal...great adventure...explore	Travelling across and out of the country is relatively cheap...make the most of your time abroad to visit

Part 7		Key words from the questions	Clues from the text
43	C	...artists who started playing musical instruments...very young age	Linzi Stoppard has been playing the violin since the age of four / Similarly, Ben Lee started playing the violin when he was five years old.
44	D	...perform anywhere in the country	Gem is happy to travel all over the UK
45	B	...singing and dancing performance	...vocal talent...and cool dance routines
46	A	...needs to spend time with the guests before	...start by joining the staff / ...give them the chance to assess the audience and to build rapport with the guests
47	C	...doesn't mention the duration	A: 30-minute performance / B: as long as 90 minutes / D: almost two-and-a-half-hour performance
48	B	...formed by women only	...all-female energetic act
49	C	...extremely expensive musical instruments	...electric violins, each worth over one million dollars
50	D	...multi-talented artist	...professional solo singer, guitar player and songwriter
51	A	...artists shock the guests with an unexpected performance	...add a surprise element to your party.
52	B	...cover group...different elements...unique performance	...the only tribute act of its kind / combine vocal talent, themed costumes and cool dance routines

Answers   Cambridge B2 First Reading   Test 7

Part 5		Key words from the questions	Clues from the text
31	D	...first paragraph...feel / ...nervous and agitated	...difficult to keep calm and hide hundreds of thoughts going through my mind / I started biting my nails and suddenly the stool I was sitting on felt incredibly uncomfortable / Darius, on the other hand, appeared calm and collected
32	D	...second paragraph...compare the host to a robot / ...general behaviour wasn't spontaneous and seemed unnatural.	...scripted lines and well-practised movements, all planned in advance by the production team
33	A	... 'both'...line 20 / The writer and her husband	...life by the sea for me and my husband. / ...slower pace of life and a peaceful lifestyle
34	B	...third paragraph...Darius change his behaviour / ...doesn't know the correct answer	For the first time, Darius looked confused and his hands were shaking / ...he had lost his confidence. He kept staring at the five options on his screen with a worried look on his face / ...randomly picked one of the options and it was clear that he was just trying to guess / ...he had chosen the wrong answer
35	C	...paragraph four...answer all the questions / ...she loves being famous	...because I still enjoyed being the centre of attention.
36	C	...fourth paragraph...life-long dream / ...by the seaside	...house on the beach that I had always wanted

Part 6		Key words from the questions	Clues from the text
37	B	Similarly, sharing...tremendous advances in education	...advantage / ...the fastest, most reliable and most accessible / ...facilitates learning and teaching
38	D	With that in mind...companies rely on influencers' videos to promote their brand.	...the ideal space to advertise all sorts of products and services / This is really a win-win situation for the company...for the influencer...
39	C	On the other hand...social media can have a negative impact	[previous paragraph talked about advantages] / ...seriously affect
40	G	Cyberbullying...embarrass or threaten others	Online bullying... / ...attacks
41	E	...difficult to find out who is committing the offence / ...victim finds the courage to talk to an adult	...common mainly among social platform users /... making cyberbullying a crime.
42	A	online dishonest scheme ...criminals...technologically skilled	cybercrime

Part 7		Key words from the questions	Clues from the text
43	B	...examples...physical movements	...body language, gestures and facial expressions.
44	C	...tracking communication as a unique feature	Unlike any other type...this one provides a record
45	D	...mainly used to assist the other types	Visual communication is often used to support other types of communication
46	A	...a skill that should be developed...to advance one type of communication	...if you want to be a good communicator, you should also improve your listening abilities
47	C	...technology has affected the most	...recent years...written communication has increased...emails, texts messages and chats
48	B	...spontaneous or controlled	...can be intentional, when you smile while greeting a customer at work for example, or unintentional, like crossing your arms when feeling uncomfortable.
49	D	...needs a variety of items	Photographs are great tools / Drawings and diagrams can be useful when photographs aren't suitable / Graphs, maps and tables are ideal for presenting data / ...objects...models / ...videos
50	A	...discourages...specific words	...filler words, such as 'like', 'uhm', 'yeah', should be avoided
51	B	...opposite meanings within the same message	...ensuring that our verbal and nonverbal communication convey the same meaning...avoid sending contrasting messages
52	C	...someone else should check the message	...ask someone you trust to check it too

Answers   Cambridge B2 First Reading   Test 8

Part 5		Key words from the questions	Clues from the text
31	C	...paragraph 1...his wife / ...too much food	...carried away / ...feeding the whole town / ...five...bags / ...more than...of two people
32	B	...'it'...line 9 / ...habit...large amounts of food	...used to buying as much as my fridge and kitchen cupboards could take / I grew up watching my mother doing the same / ...that's where I
33	D	Second paragraph...feels / ...glad...husband isn't shopping	I wouldn't have wanted him by my side while filling up my trolley / ...turning a usually pleasant experience into a stressful one
34	A	...paragraph 3...describe their shopping day / Well organised and predictable	Every payday / ...I would spend about 45 minutes to one hour... / I would send him a text...he would pick me up and / ...we would unpack our groceries together and store them properly
35	B	...fourth paragraph...doesn't understand / why...buying so much more than usual	...people were panic-buying for groceries / I struggled to find a reason for this...
36	A	...paragraph 5...husband behave outside / ...chatty and cheerful	...attempt to lighten the atmosphere, my husband tried to start a conversation / ...he even managed to make a few people smile with his jokes

Part 6		Key words from the questions	Clues from the text
37	F	...irresponsible behaviour...issues for vulnerable and elderly...weren't able to get the supplies they needed	...fear of food shortages /...crowded the supermarkets to stock up on essentials
38	E	In the meantime...reduce the problems caused by panic-buyers...dedicating specific shopping hours to customers over 60	While...staff worked hard at replenishing the shelves...protected the older population
39	A	...voluntary groups spontaneously popped up all over the world...emotional and practical support...generosity and compassion...features in mankind	Despite...unkind and greedy actions, communities worldwide...to help those in need / ...who make an effort to put others first and to show that kindness...global community
40	G	Surprisingly...the response was so big that this group expanded	...started by distributing leaflets / Her group was set up...volunteers were asked to join in.
41	D	closure of businesses...job losses	...financially affected...were struggling / ...who have lost their jobs and find it difficult to provide for their families
42	B	Not only groups...individuals...help others	[First part of the paragraph talks about groups] / Yoga and fitness instructors...promote physical activity...while tourist guides...keeping company to those stuck at home

Part 7		Key words from the questions	Clues from the text
43	B	...keeping our distance...protect older people	...stay away from vulnerable people, such as the elderly
44	C	...good hygiene in a domestic and professional environment	At home and at work, we should clean and disinfect objects and surfaces that are touched or used frequently, such as...
45	A	...how...keep fingers and palms clean	...we should wash our hands / ...use soap and water / ...use hand sanitisers
46	D	...countries...stop to this pandemic	...governments worldwide have taken a course of action to fight the spreading of the virus / Some countries...stricter measures than others
47	B	...electronic devices...individuals...maintain contact with family and friends	...keeping in touch with loved ones / ...advanced technology ...alternative to face-to-face communication
48	D	...scheme...health and the financial stability of the population	...a plan that should protect the physical, mental and economic well-being of all citizens
49	B	...have to become flexible...how...connect with others	...we have to learn new ways to socialise
50	D	...lists...day-to-day activities...might be affected	A pandemic can have an impact on everyone's daily life, from public transport, to social interaction, to work/study routine.
51	C	...infected people...behave	...the measures are even stricter if we feel unwell / ...recover at home, but we should do our best / We should stay in an allocated 'sick' room and wear a face mask
52	A	...items that might work as barriers	...wearing plastic gloves and face masks hoping to further shield themselves

PROSPERITY EDUCATION
www.prosperityeducation.net

Cambridge B2 First Use of English: Parts 1–4

Sample content taken from

Use of English:
ten practice tests for the Cambridge B2 First

by Michael Macdonald

Cambridge B2 First Use of English: Parts 1–4

Test 1

Cambridge B2 First Use of English

For questions 1–8, read the text below and decide which answer best fits each gap. In the separate answer sheet, mark the appropriate answer (A, B, C or D).

Madrid

Madrid has been the capital of Spain since 1677. **(1)**_____ there has been a **(2)**_____ on the site since prehistoric times, the city is first mentioned in historical documents dating from the 9th century. Madrid´s **(3)**_____ shows one of the many bears that used to be found in the local forests in the Middle Ages eating from a locally grown madroño tree. The city **(4)**_____ in the geographical centre of Spain.

The community of Madrid has a **(5)**_____ of some 6 million people. It boasts a modern public transport system and international airport; it has several wonderful public parks and **(6)**_____ of the best art museums in the world. You would be well advised to take in the Picassos at the Reina Sofia Museum or **(7)**_____ a visit to the Prado Museum to see the works of Velazquez, among others.

For those who are more interested in popular culture, Madrid offers wonderful shopping on any of the streets on or off Gran Via, the **(8)**_____ street.

1	**A**	However	**B**	Although	**C**	Because	**D**	Whereas
2	**A**	camp	**B**	settlement	**C**	establishment	**D**	foundation
3	**A**	image	**B**	emblem	**C**	brand	**D**	name
4	**A**	lies	**B**	exists	**C**	locates	**D**	reaches
5	**A**	people	**B**	volume	**C**	total	**D**	population
6	**A**	any	**B**	some	**C**	much	**D**	few
7	**A**	do	**B**	pay	**C**	have	**D**	find
8	**A**	grand	**B**	big	**C**	main	**D**	key

For questions 9–16, read the text below and decide which word best fits each gap. Use only one word for each gap. In the separate answer sheet, write your answers in capital letters, using one box per letter.

Born to rock

I am the lead guitarist **(1)**_____ a rock band. When I was a young girl I **(2)**_____ to a concert where the music was so loud it hurt my ears. I loved every moment and, when the band finished playing and **(3)**_____ crowd screamed for more, I knew then what I wanted to do with my life.

I started **(4)**_____ the guitar and worked at it really hard all through my teenage years. When I finished school, I went **(5)**_____ university where I studied Music (classical guitar) and Music Technology, the science of recording sound. I learnt a **(6)**_____ about the technical side of music and performance.

Now, when I **(7)**_____ not playing guitar in my band, I teach children **(8)**_____ to play. Music is in my blood, and I was born to rock.

For questions 17–24, use the stem word on the right to form the correct word that fills each gap. In the separate answer sheet, write your answers in capital letters, using one box per letter.

Madrid

My first job, after I left school, was in a call-centre in Dublin, Ireland. At the time, there was plenty of work in the 'teleworking' industry, due to a recent increase in mobile phone **(17)**_____. My role was to provide telephone numbers to people who **(18)**_____ 192 from their handsets. They would come through to me and tell me the name of the person or business they wished to be **(19)**_____ to. I would then select the appropriate number from a large database and put them through, **(20)**_____ sure to be polite all the time.

It must be **(21)**_____ that I did not like that job very much: the hours were long (I worked a 12-hour night shift, from 9pm to 9am), the environment was **(22)**_____ busy and the pay was not very good. However, that call-centre was where I met my future wife. In fact, I was her manager! At first, we did not connect: she thought I was boring, and I thought she was **(23)**_____, but, after some time, we ended up developing a close **(24)**_____. Then, one morning, after our long shift, we walked home together and stopped for a coffee.

The rest, as they say, is history…

OWNER

DIAL

CONNECT

MAKE

ACKNOWLEDGE

EXTREME

ANNOY

FRIEND

For questions 25–30, complete the second sentence, using the word given, so that it has a similar meaning to the first sentence. Do not change the word provided and use between two and five words in total. In the separate answer sheet, write your answers in capital letters, using one box per letter.

25 The driver said we were going to be late.

AS

"I´m sorry to say it _____ are going to be late", said the driver.

26 You must call beforehand to reserve time with the therapist.

MAKE

You have _____ see the therapist before you come.

27 It is a shame you weren´t able to be more understanding about his problem.

COULD

I think _____ more understanding about his problem.

28 I described the problem to him in detail.

DETAILED

I _____ of the problem.

29 Very few people were at the match on Saturday.

CAME

Hardly _____ the match on Saturday.

30 Because the exam was so easy more pupils passed than expected.

DUE

More pupils passed than expected _____ so easy.

Part 1: Multiple choice						
1	B	Although	5	D	population	
2	B	settlement	6	B	some	
3	B	emblem	7	B	pay	
4	A	lies	8	C	main	

Part 2: Open cloze			
9	in	13	to
10	went	14	lot
11	the	15	am
12	playing/learning	16	how

Part 3: Word formation			
17	ownership	21	acknowledged
18	dialled	22	extremely
19	connected	23	annoying
20	making	24	friendship

Part 4: Key word transformation		
25	appears/seems/looks	as though we/as if we
26	to make	an appointment to
27	you could	have been
28	gave him	a detailed description
29	anyone/anybody	came to/came to watch
30	due to	the exam being/it being

Answer sheet: Cambridge B2 First Use of English

Test No. ☐

Mark out of 36 ☐

Name _____ Date _____

Part 1: Multiple choice   8 marks

Mark the appropriate answer (A, B, C or D).

| 0 | A | **B** | C | D | |

1	A	B	C	D		5	A	B	C	D
2	A	B	C	D		6	A	B	C	D
3	A	B	C	D		7	A	B	C	D
4	A	B	C	D		8	A	B	C	D

Part 2: Open cloze   8 marks

Write your answers in capital letters, using one box per letter.

| 0 | B | E | C | A | U | S | E | | | | |

9											
10											
11											
12											
13											
14											
15											
16											

Answer sheet: Cambridge B2 First Use of English

Part 3: Word formation

8 marks

Write your answers in capital letters, using one box per letter.

17 ⬜⬜⬜⬜⬜⬜⬜⬜⬜⬜⬜⬜

18 ⬜⬜⬜⬜⬜⬜⬜⬜⬜⬜⬜⬜

19 ⬜⬜⬜⬜⬜⬜⬜⬜⬜⬜⬜⬜

20 ⬜⬜⬜⬜⬜⬜⬜⬜⬜⬜⬜⬜

21 ⬜⬜⬜⬜⬜⬜⬜⬜⬜⬜⬜⬜

22 ⬜⬜⬜⬜⬜⬜⬜⬜⬜⬜⬜⬜

23 ⬜⬜⬜⬜⬜⬜⬜⬜⬜⬜⬜⬜

24 ⬜⬜⬜⬜⬜⬜⬜⬜⬜⬜⬜⬜

50% discount code: 050DAUQ0

Part 4: Key word transformation

12 marks

Write your answers in capital letters, using one box per letter.

25 ⬜⬜⬜⬜⬜⬜⬜⬜⬜⬜⬜⬜⬜⬜⬜⬜⬜⬜⬜⬜
   ⬜⬜⬜⬜⬜⬜⬜⬜⬜⬜⬜⬜⬜⬜⬜⬜⬜⬜⬜

26 ⬜⬜⬜⬜⬜⬜⬜⬜⬜⬜⬜⬜⬜⬜⬜⬜⬜⬜⬜⬜
   ⬜⬜⬜⬜⬜⬜⬜⬜⬜⬜⬜⬜⬜⬜⬜⬜⬜⬜⬜

27 ⬜⬜⬜⬜⬜⬜⬜⬜⬜⬜⬜⬜⬜⬜⬜⬜⬜⬜⬜⬜
   ⬜⬜⬜⬜⬜⬜⬜⬜⬜⬜⬜⬜⬜⬜⬜⬜⬜⬜⬜

28 ⬜⬜⬜⬜⬜⬜⬜⬜⬜⬜⬜⬜⬜⬜⬜⬜⬜⬜⬜⬜
   ⬜⬜⬜⬜⬜⬜⬜⬜⬜⬜⬜⬜⬜⬜⬜⬜⬜⬜⬜

29 ⬜⬜⬜⬜⬜⬜⬜⬜⬜⬜⬜⬜⬜⬜⬜⬜⬜⬜⬜⬜
   ⬜⬜⬜⬜⬜⬜⬜⬜⬜⬜⬜⬜⬜⬜⬜⬜⬜⬜⬜

30 ⬜⬜⬜⬜⬜⬜⬜⬜⬜⬜⬜⬜⬜⬜⬜⬜⬜⬜⬜⬜
   ⬜⬜⬜⬜⬜⬜⬜⬜⬜⬜⬜⬜⬜⬜⬜⬜⬜⬜⬜

www.prosperityeducation.net

Cambridge B2 First Use of English: Parts 1–4

Test 6

Cambridge B2 First Use of English

For questions 1–8, read the text below and decide which answer best fits each gap. In the separate answer sheet, mark the appropriate answer (A, B, C or D).

A whale of a time

I guess I've got a **(1)**_____ weird hobby. At **(2)**_____, I thought that until I read that more than ten million people do the same thing every year. Of course, most of those people will only do it once, whereas I've made a habit of it. It's something you can do in almost **(3)**_____ country in the world, so long as they have a coastline. What am I talking about? Whale-watching, obviously!

My first 'whale watch' was in the town of Hermanus, in South Africa, where there is a 'whale crier' **(4)**_____ job is to attract the attention of tourists when whales are sighted **(5)**_____. My first whale was a Southern Right Whale. They grow to around 16 metres in length (half the size of an adult Blue Whale). Now I try to see whales at least once a year, and my hobby has **(6)**_____ me to Portugal, Norway and England. I'm saving up for a **(7)**_____ to Iceland next year. It will be expensive but I'm planning on finally seeing my first Blue Whale, the true **(8)**_____ of the ocean.

1	A	almost	B	completely	C	nearly	D	pretty
2	A	least	B	most	C	all	D	it
3	A	every	B	all	C	total	D	none
4	A	own	B	whose	C	that	D	which
5	A	beside	B	nearby	C	by	D	near
6	A	travelled	B	pulled	C	taken	D	lifted
7	A	trip	B	spot	C	travel	D	journey
8	A	beast	B	huge	C	giant	D	mammoth

For questions 9–16, read the text below and decide which word best fits each gap. Use only one word for each gap. In the separate answer sheet, write your answers in capital letters, using one box per letter.

The World Wide Web

Don't **(9)**_____ the internet and the World Wide Web confused. Put simply, the internet is a global network of computers, while the World Wide Web is an information system that operates within that network.

The World Wide Web is now ever-present in modern society. It is sometimes difficult to remember that **(10)**_____ upon a time, and not so long ago, it didn't exist and needed to be invented **(11)**_____ someone. That someone was Tim Berners-Lee, an English computer scientist.

Berners-Lee, the son of two mathematicians, **(12)**_____ born in 1955 in England. He studied Physics at Oxford University and originally worked **(13)**_____ the idea as a side project for organising his own data, but he did not immediately recognise its full potential. **(14)**_____ a couple of years, he abandoned the project to work on other ideas. It was **(15)**_____ after an incubation period of about ten years, in 1989, that Berners-Lee was able to visualise the great possibilities of his work and finally turn the World Wide Web **(16)**_____ a reality.

For questions 17–24, use the stem word on the right to form the correct word that fills each gap. In the separate answer sheet, write your answers in capital letters, using one box per letter.

The story of market research

When the Curtis Publishing Company **(17)**_____ Charles Coolidge Parlin to research its markets, the aim was to show how advertisements can improve sales, and to therefore, **(18)**_____, sell more advertising space in its publications. This initial research is widely recognised as the birth of 'Market Research', a **(19)**_____ industry that currently employs half a million people in the USA alone.

COMMISSION

HOPE

GLOBE

This act marked an important change from a 'producer-led' approach to business, where companies produced things and then tried to get people to buy them, to a 'consumer-led' **(20)**_____, in which companies take the time to ask the general public what *they* want and *then* find ways to produce whatever it is in the hope of **(21)**_____ them into customers.

MENTAL

TURN

Market research is fundamental to modern commerce. It is the process of harvesting our data and deriving from it our consumer habits and **(22)**_____, be it a questionnaire we fill out, the social media platform we populate, or the supermarket **(23)**_____ card we carry around. Today, the practice of advertising has become streamlined and more targeted, and, therefore, **(24)**_____ more effective.

PREFER

LOYAL

DOUBT

Cambridge B2 First Use of English

Part 4   Key word transformation   Test 6

For questions 25–30, complete the second sentence, using the word given, so that it has a similar meaning to the first sentence. Do not change the word provided and use between two and five words in total. In the separate answer sheet, write your answers in capital letters, using one box per letter.

25   "How long is the swimming pool?", asked Jenny.

      WHAT

      Jenny asked _____ of the swimming pool was.

26   The children washed John´s car.

      HAD

      John _____ by the children.

27   "Piotr! You have eaten all the cake!", said Piotr's mum.

      ACCUSED

      Piotr's mum _____ all the cake.

28   Marina didn´t hear the answer because she wasn´t listening.

      PAYING

      If Marina had _____ have heard the answer.

29   You should not have taken that book without asking.

      OUGHT

      You _____ borrowing that book.

30   I spent ages doing my homework.

      TOOK

      It _____ my homework.

Part 1: Multiple choice					
1	D	pretty	5	B	nearby
2	A	least	6	C	taken
3	A	every	7	A	trip
4	B	whose	8	C	giant

Part 2: Open cloze			
9	get	13	on
10	once	14	After
11	by	15	only
12	was	16	into

Part 3: Word formation			
17	commissioned	21	turning
18	hopefully	22	preferences
19	global	23	loyalty
20	mentality	24	undoubtedly

Part 4: Key word transformation		
25	what	the length
26	had his	car washed
27	accused him/accused Piotr	of eating/of having eaten
28	been paying attention	she would/she might
29	ought to	have asked before
30	took me ages	to do/to complete/to finish

Answer sheet: Cambridge B2 First Use of English

Test No. [ ]

Mark out of 36 [ ]

Name _____ Date _____

Part 1: Multiple choice   8 marks

Mark the appropriate answer (A, B, C or D).

| 0 | A | B | C | D | |

1	A	B	C	D		5	A	B	C	D
2	A	B	C	D		6	A	B	C	D
3	A	B	C	D		7	A	B	C	D
4	A	B	C	D		8	A	B	C	D

Part 2: Open cloze   8 marks

Write your answers in capital letters, using one box per letter.

| 0 | B | E | C | A | U | S | E | | | | |

9										
10										
11										
12										
13										
14										
15										
16										

Answer sheet: Cambridge B2 First Use of English

Part 3: Word formation

8 marks

Write your answers in capital letters, using one box per letter.

17												
18												
19												
20												
21												
22												
23												
24												

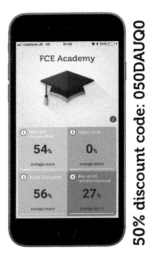

50% discount code: 050DAUQ0

Part 4: Key word transformation

12 marks

Write your answers in capital letters, using one box per letter.

25																				
26																				
27																				
28																				
29																				
30																				

Notes

Notes

Notes

Notes